Christmas Memories at Waterside Cottage

K.T. DADY

Christmas Memories at Waterside Cottage
Published by K.T. Dady

Copyright © 2023 K.T. Dady

All rights reserved.
No part of this book may be reproduced or used in any manner whatsoever without the express written permission of the author, except for the use of brief quotations in a book review.

This is a work of fiction. Names, characters, places, and incidents are the product of the author's imagination or, if real, are used fictitiously.

Cover design by K.T. Dady.
Cover photography: Canva.

Some people are worth remembering.

1

Grace

Ooh, my head hurts. Why is my throat so dry? What's that bleeping noise? Who is that talking? Is that Freddy?

Grace slowly opened her eyes, blinked a couple of times, waited patiently for her blurred vision to clear, and then glanced down at the hospital bed she was lying in. The smell of school dinners was lurking in the air, and whispered words were coming from the far end of her room. She was about to wonder why she was in hospital when she noticed something else that took priority.

Her sister Molly was curled up on Freddy Morland's lap in a large blue chair in the corner of the room. Grace raised her head a touch and squinted her eyes. She blinked hard, then focused back on her little sister. Even stretching her eyelids as wide as they could go made no difference. What she was seeing was definitely there all right. Molly and Freddy were locked in a gentle kiss, and the world around them had obviously buggered off, including Grace.

What the hell is my sister doing kissing my boyfriend?

Grace went to yell out to Freddy, but somehow her voice box hadn't quite got the memo. She coughed, choked on air, and tried to sit up so quickly her head started to spin. Something was attached to the back of her hand that wasn't normally there, and it jolted her sideways. A clanking noise echoed in her ears, and voices were close by whilst hands were forcing her back to the plump white pillow behind her neck.

Everything turned black for a moment before her senses returned in full force, revealing a weak body and a frazzled mind.

Am I dreaming? What's happening here?

Grace's eyelids felt heavy, but she opened them anyway. The first face she saw was Molly. At least, she looked like Molly, but close up, she looked a bit older than normal. Not by much, but there was definitely some change. Her sister's complexion wasn't as pink as it usually was. In fact, Molly looked quite washed-out and seemed stressed as the smallest of smiles broke out on her face.

Oh, you want to smile at me? You think I didn't just see you snogging my boyfriend?

At least, that's what she thought she saw. She wasn't quite sure what to think.

Freddy's face came into view, peering down, examining her from head to toe with his caramel eyes that kept going in and out of focus. She followed one of his apricot curls as it flopped down his forehead to bounce upon his right eyebrow. Normally she would reach out and gently push it back.

There wasn't much energy flowing through Grace's body, but somehow she managed to lift her arm and lightly brush her fingertips across Freddy's cheekbone, resting there for two seconds. Then, using the last remaining drop of energy she had about her being, she slapped his face, which ended up more of a tap, but he got the message.

Freddy jumped back as Molly gasped. Grace's arm flopped to the bed whilst her sister waffled on about Freddy's well-being, Grace's state of mind, and something to do with a doctor.

A hand was suddenly under her head, lifting her mouth towards a cup of warm water, which tasted like metal, and she wasn't sure if Molly was now trying to poison her just to cover her backstabbing tracks. She tried to move away, causing the water to spill down her chin. Her sister mumbled something she couldn't make out, then her head was replaced on the pillow.

Somehow words needed to form, because there was far too much to say, and even if it was some sort of bizarre dream, Grace was determined to be in control of some parts, mainly the part about her boyfriend cheating on her with her sister, of all people.

Grace loved her family with all her heart and was always there for her five younger sisters, no matter what. Somebody must have drugged her, or Molly, either way, something was amiss. There was no way Molly would hurt her like that. She had to know the truth. Where she was. The kissing in the corner. Why she was so weak.

'Molly…'

'Shh, Grace. Don't try to talk. Just rest. The doctor is on his way.' Molly started faffing around the bed covers and pillows whilst looking half worried and half relieved. She kept saying over and over that everything was going to be all right to the point Grace had Bob Marley stuck in her head.

Grace then heard Freddy's voice again. He was talking to someone else, someone whose footsteps were rapidly approaching her bed.

The most gorgeous face peered down at her with a look of concern that quickly faded to one of pure adoration.

'Hey, you.' His voice was so soft, Grace felt it soothe her soul.

Ooh, hot doc alert. And he has an accent. American, maybe? Who cares, he doesn't need to speak. I don't need to hear him at all. So, you, Freddy Morland, can bugger right off.

As far as she was concerned, Molly could have Freddy. She was going to settle right there in her bizarre dream and simply stare at the fine specimen of a man smiling her way.

Grace relaxed as the doctor placed the back of his hand lightly on her cheek. She closed her eyes, ready for another nap, hoping his caring touch didn't fade away with her crazy dream. His hand moved, and she missed it already. Her eyes slowly opened to peer up into the dark-blue ones looking back. A wide smile, revealing perfect teeth, spread across his face as he once again touched her, this time to brush her hair back from her forehead.

My goodness, your smile is cute.

She wondered if doctors normally looked at their patients in such a way, then figured he was probably studying her eyes for signs of the Yellow Brick Road, because she sure as hell wasn't in Kansas anymore.

The doctor leaned closer and gently nudged her nose with his own, and although his public display of affection felt quite nice, Grace was pretty sure that kind of act wasn't standard medical procedure. In fact, it was just plain weird.

'Molly,' croaked Grace, desperately trying to find the one person around her who she felt safe with, even if she had just stabbed her directly in the heart.

Molly came into view, moving Hot Doc to one side. 'I'm here, Gracie.' She let out a loud sigh, sounding tense. 'I'm so glad you're back. Mum and Dad are on their way. Well, everyone is, but Fred called them first. How are you feeling?'

Grace's eyes flittered around the room. The tall doctor was standing at the foot of her bed, reading her chart and talking to a nurse. Freddy was on the phone to someone, and Molly suddenly had tears in her eyes.

Yeah, you can cry. I hope you do feel guilty. Kissing Freddy while I'm lying here in hospital...

'Why am I in hospital, Molls?'

'You were in an accident, Grace. You got knocked down by a car.' Molly gave her hand a gentle squeeze whilst blinking away tears. 'You gave us all a right scare.' She rested her head upon Grace's shoulder for a beat, then raised herself to kiss her cheek. 'I love you, Gracie. Don't ever do that again.'

Grace took a deep breath, ignoring the scratchy feeling at the back of her throat. 'Come closer, Molls.'

Molly leaned over so her ear was facing Grace's mouth. 'What is it?'

'Why the hell were you just kissing my boyfriend?'

Molly's dark eyes widened as she straightened to glance over at the doctor, who had stopped talking to the nurse and was staring at Grace as though she had said something peculiar.

Grace was questioning herself. Maybe her words didn't come out as she had heard them. Everyone in the room was staring at her as though she had three heads. Something was definitely wrong.

Molly swallowed hard. 'Erm... I didn't kiss Charlie.' Her worried eyes flittered over to Freddy before landing on the doctor.

Charlie? Have they drugged me? I need to wake up, or sleep. I'm not sure.

Grace wished her mum was there to sort everything.

Hot Doc was back. His concerned face was peering down at her again. 'Hey, Grace. Can you tell me what day it is?'

Erm... I was coming out the Donkey Sanctuary. Yeah, that's right. I was leaving work for the day. When was that? What day is it today?

'Wednesday, I think.'

The cute smile was back, only not as wide as before. 'That's okay. What about your full name. Can you tell me what it is?'

'Grace Elizabeth Hadley.' She looked at Molly for confirmation, then wondered why. Molly just smiled warmly whilst nodding her head slightly.

'And how old are you, Grace?'

'Twenty-nine.'

Grace felt the energy in the room change. Something was off, way more than the stale dinner smell in the air. The doctor flashed a light in her eyes and then told her to follow his finger. He spoke to the nurse again before leaving the room.

'It's okay, Grace,' said Molly, trying to be reassuring, but Grace could see her nerves.

'Molly, what's going on?'

'You hit your head. It kind of knocked you out for a bit.'

'How long is a bit?'

Molly's lips clamped tightly together as she made a humming noise, which was something she used to do as a kid whenever she was deep in thought. Grace wondered what exactly Molly had to think so deeply about. 'Three weeks.'

Grey sparkles filled Grace's eyes for a few seconds before blackness took over, wiping her out for what she assumed was a moment. When she woke, Freddy had disappeared, and Molly was talking to the doctor.

'Hey, Grace, you're awake.' Molly rushed over and grabbed her hand. 'It's okay. You're going to be fine. We're just waiting for another doctor to arrive.'

Hot Doc stepped closer. He wasn't smiling, but Grace could see warmth in his eyes. She tried to figure out what colour blue they were. They weren't like her shade of clear sea blue. All her sisters had a similar shade, except Molly. She was the only one with dark eyes, which caused many jokes over the years. Hot Doc had eyes the colour of the sky just before it turned to night. Grace imagined a sun setting somewhere back there. He looked like the sunset. Warm, tranquil, beautiful. His hair was jet black, his skin tone a shade lighter than olive, and there was something familiar about him that she couldn't quite put her finger on.

'Grace, do you know who I am?' he asked softly.

'The doctor?' She couldn't see a name badge or lanyard or anything, so she kind of questioned her judgment for a moment, seeing he had asked.

He smiled ever so slightly. 'That's right. I'm a doctor. I'm Dr Wallis. Charlie Wallis.'

Molly squeezed her hand again. 'It's Charlie.'

Grace wasn't sure why her sister was acting like she should know that. She couldn't be expected to know every doctor in the hospital. She'd only just woken up from three weeks…

Wait, three weeks!

'Three weeks, Molls. I've been asleep for that long?'

Molly gently patted her fingers. 'You were in a coma, Grace. You had a little bit of swelling on the brain. Nothing to worry about. You're going to be all right now, but we think you might need a bit longer to heal. Your memory is playing up, that's all. You'll probably be back to normal after a good night's sleep.'

'You just said I've been asleep for three weeks. How much more sleep do I need? And what's wrong with my memory? I know who you are, don't I? Are you trying to gaslight me because you don't want me remembering you kissing Freddy?' Grace looked over at Charlie. 'When I woke up, my little sister was snogging my boyfriend. Can you believe that, Dr Wallis?'

'Freddy's not your boyfriend anymore.' Molly held a sympathetic smile, which only irritated Grace.

I gathered that much when I saw him locked in an embrace with you.

Molly sighed quietly and started to fiddle with the middle button on her blue cardigan. 'You broke up four years ago. You never loved each other, so you both decided it was for the best to just go back to being friends.'

'That's convenient for you, Molly.'

'It's true, Grace. You only dated for two months before calling it a day. You were always such good friends, that's why you both tried dating after you both got hurt by other people, but it wasn't right for either of you. You both laugh about it whenever it comes up. You're still really good mates. Although, I'm not sure now since you smacked him in the face.'

'Two months? But we've only been together one month. You're not making any sense.'

Charlie gave Molly a look that pretty much told Grace the doctor was telling her sister to take it easy. Grace turned his way to see those smiling eyes focus solely on her.

'Dr Wallis, have I really lost my memory?'

'It seems that way at the moment, but you've only just woken from a coma. These things take time.'

Grace touched her head, feeling for a wound. 'So, I'm not with Freddy? It's not September? And is that why Molly looks a bit older than she did yesterday, or whenever I last saw her? Wait... So, I'm not twenty-nine? How old am I?'

Molly grinned. 'You're thirty-three, you old woman.' She laughed, which made Grace almost smile at the absurdity. 'Don't worry though, you still look good.'

'Are you telling me I can't remember four years of my life?' Shock alone was stopping her from bursting into tears.

'It'll come back,' said Charlie. His expression changed when he looked over at Molly. It was almost as if he was willing Grace's memory to return to sender as he added, 'It has to.'

Grace breathed out a sore laugh. 'So, still single then.'

Molly shook her head. 'No, my lovely, you're married.'

It was definitely a dream. Now she was one hundred percent sure. One of those real-life dreams, or nightmares. She couldn't decide which she was in, but it was absolutely a dream. There was no way she would forget getting married. Forgetting stuff about Freddy, yeah, easy. But marriage. No way.

This is nuts.

Grace glanced at her bare wedding finger. 'I think I would remember getting married, Molls.'

Molly nodded fervently. 'And you will. Tomorrow. Once you've had time to come around. Your mind needs some more time to catch up.'

'Catch up? Are you kidding me? I've just woken up in hospital. I don't remember being hit by a car. Three weeks have passed, and four years, it would appear. I'm no longer dating Freddy, I'm in my thirties, and now I'm married?' She watched her sister purse her lips and silently nod. 'To who? Who did I marry?' She followed Molly's eyes over to Charlie. Neither of them spoke, so she looked back at her sister as her stomach swirled as though she were on a roller coaster. 'Tell me, Molly. Who?'

Molly gestured across the bed. 'Him, Grace. You're married to Charlie Wallis.'

Grace's eyes nearly popped straight out of her head. 'I'm married to Hot Doc?' All other words failed her.

Charlie grinned, then bit his bottom lip. 'Ah, so that was your secret name for me.'
Oh my bloody God!

2

Charlie

Charlie tried quite a few times to explain everything the neurologist, Dr Singh, had told him about Grace. But her parents were struggling to understand, even though he'd simplified every word. He silently sighed with his own frustrations. His wife had no memory of him and that hurt so much. She couldn't remember their first encounter, date, or even the day they married, but right now, all that mattered was her family coming to terms with the fact that the missing last four years of Grace's life might never return.

He gazed around the room, then rested his eyes on the picture of a summer garden at the back of the small office that had somehow managed to squeeze in Grace's parents and all five of her sisters.

The second eldest, Ashley, was trying to calm her mother by wiping her tears and stroking her back. 'It's okay, Mum. The most important thing is that our Gracie is alive.'

The youngest sister had dyed white-blonde hair cut into short layers, and Charlie perused the small wispy bits sticking up on top of her head as she joined in the conversation that had finally quietened a touch. 'The doctor never said her memory wouldn't return at all. Charlie just explained that it might not. Might is not a definite.'

'Kerri's right,' said Molly. 'No one knows how these things go. Everyone is different.' She looked over at Charlie, giving him a reassuring smile and a slight nod of the head. 'Grace will make a full recovery very soon, right, Charlie?'

He stopped focusing on Kerri's hair and looked back down at Grace's mum, still sobbing in the chair opposite his desk. He handed another tissue to Ashley, who gave it to her mum. 'Whatever happens, Fiona, we'll get Grace through it.'

Fiona sniffed and blew her nose. Her arm wriggled free of Ashley's hold and reached out towards her husband to hold his hand. 'I know. Our baby is a strong girl. Always has been. She'll be all right, won't she, Ronnie?'

Grace's dad appeared to be holding it together more than anyone else in the room. He sat up straight, brushed his salt-and-pepper hair back, and pursed his thin lips. 'She's going to be just fine, Fee. There's no need for anyone to worry. Her memory will be one of the ones that comes back. She just needs more time. It's early days, and she's not in familiar surroundings.'

'Ooh, that's a good point,' said another sister. 'Once she's out of here, it'll all come back to her. She won't be my age for much longer, which is a shame, I always wanted a twin.'

Fiona tightened her brow as she turned to scorn her daughter. 'This is no time for jokes, Lexi.'

Lexi lowered her shoulders and huffed quietly. 'Mum, this is exactly how we need to be when we face Grace. We can't come at her with doom and gloom all over our faces. She needs us to be us, and that means making the jokes we do. Dad just said about things being familiar, well, that includes how we are as a family. Grace will expect light, love, and humour. We can't start walking on eggshells and wrapping her in cotton wool. She won't know where she's at if we change our ways.'

All the other sisters nodded as Ronnie gently tapped his wife's knuckles. 'Lexi's right, Fee. If we're going to bring our baby home, then home is what she'll get. She'll heal faster that way.'

What's he talking about, bringing her home? She lives with me. They're not taking her back to their house, are they? Is that what they have planned? Surely not.

Charlie swallowed hard, feeling uncomfortable for the first time since meeting the Hadleys. Even when Grace had taken him home for his first meet and greet, he wasn't as nervous as he was now. 'We need to talk about Grace going home, Ron.'

Ronnie flapped one hand his way. 'It's all in hand, son. You don't have to worry about a thing. We've got plenty of room now the others have all moved out. Well, Kerri's still got some of her stuff to shift, but that's not in the way.' He turned to her. 'Still, it wouldn't hurt for you to get a wriggle on, love.'

Kerri frowned at her father as she shuffled in her chair.

Harriet, the fifth daughter, had been the quietest since they all gathered for the long-awaited chat about Grace's condition. She shifted in her chair by the window and turned her head away from her view of the car park. 'I could move back in for a while with Tommy. That might help jog Grace's memory.' She glanced over at Charlie. 'Everyone was still living at home when my son was born. Tommy's pretty much grown up with his aunts always being around. I know she'll be expecting him to be… Four years ago, so that would make Tommy four, as he's just turned eight, so yeah, that'll be a shock for her, but having him around might help. Jude won't mind. We're all squashed into a small caravan on our land while our house is being built, so he'll probably be glad of a bit of extra room for a while.'

Fiona seemed to perk up. 'Well, that's not a bad idea. Ron, what do you think?'

I know what I think about these decisions being made as though I no longer exist in Grace's life. And it's not happening. I have to say something.

'I want her to come back home to Waterside Cottage, with me.'

All eyes were on him as an awkward silence filled the cinnamon, orange, and cloves faintly scented air, which came from the potpourri sitting on the windowsill that Grace had bought him the week before her accident.

Fiona cleared her throat and lightly squeezed her husband's hand, which didn't go unnoticed to Charlie. He could clearly see their silent code and knew exactly what it meant. Grace did the same to him whenever she needed his voice to take over.

Ronnie's blue eyes met Charlie with softness, firmness, and a hint of remorse. 'Son, don't you think it would make more sense for Grace to come home with us? We're her parents. We know how to look after our baby.'

'She's not a baby anymore. She's a grown woman, and a very capable one. She's missing four years, not the ability to function.'

None of the sisters made eye contact. Heads were lowered or attention focused elsewhere. Clearly, they were leaving this argument to their parents.

Fiona leaned closer to the desk and flopped her arms upon some paperwork sitting there. 'Listen, love, we're not trying to take Grace away from you. We're just doing what's best for our daughter.'

'She's my wife, and she belongs with me. That is what's best for her.'

Fiona shook her head a touch and smiled weakly. 'But she doesn't know you, Charlie.' Her tone was gentle and filled with sorrow, but all the same, her words stung. He knew she was right, but he didn't want to process that.

Ronnie looked around at his daughters before turning back to Charlie. 'Dr Singh said familiar could really help Grace—'

Ashley interrupted, 'But that might be what she finds when she goes back to Waterside, Dad. Her life is there. What if she walks through the door and everything comes flooding back?'

He nodded his approval. 'Well, that's something we could try as well.' His eyes were back on Charlie. 'But, right now, she doesn't know you from Adam, and I don't want her scared because she's been forced to live with a stranger.'

A stranger? I've been in her life for four years. We're supposed to celebrating our wedding anniversary soon. And now you want to take it all away?

He needed to think rationally, for Grace's sake. For all their sakes. 'I know she doesn't remember her life with me, but if she's not around me, how can I help her come back to me?'

Ashley raised her hand slightly, waggling one finger near her ear. 'Erm, what about if I move into the cottage with her. That way, she'll be around her own things but won't be scared.' She glanced at Charlie. 'I'm not saying she will be afraid to be alone with you, but you have to see it from her point of view. She thinks it's September in the year she's stuck in, and she didn't meet you that year until December. She doesn't know you, so living alone with you will be weird for her, right?'

Harriet looked back out at the car park. 'I think we should let Gracie decide where she wants to live.'

'I agree,' said Kerri, glancing around the room to see who was on board with that idea. Everyone nodded except her mum, who was looking reluctant. 'What's wrong, Mum?'

Fiona scrunched one shoulder up to her cheek. 'I don't know. Is Grace in the right frame of mind to be making these sorts of decisions for herself?'

Ashley turned to the door. 'I guess there's only one way to find out.'

Charlie swallowed hard. His hands were clammy and his heart rate had accelerated. He wasn't ready to hear Grace reject him. It was all too much. Since the moment he laid eyes on her, he had fallen in love. There was no way he could be parted from her, not now. Not ever. He sniffed and rolled back the tears trying to form as he watched Grace's family leave his office. He gazed down at the photograph on his desk. It was a copy of the one they had taken in a Santa booth the first year they met. A wave of gratitude washed over him at his ability to remember a moment so valuable in his life.

Snow covered the ground that day, and the sky held the softest of pinks mixed with baby blue. Late afternoon had set in, and the scent of hotdogs mingled all around him at the Sandly Christmas Market. He'd only been on the Isle of Wight two months and had settled quite easily into his new job as an A&E doctor at the hospital. An old friend from university had made sure Charlie got interviewed for the role. They had laughed at the time, making jokes about the stars aligning, because in such a short space, he had got a new job, his aunt wanted to move from Waterside Cottage, so sold it to him when she heard he was moving to the island, and then he met Grace.

December 1st. A Christmas scene. And a meet-cute that had them both enter the Santa booth at the same time from opposite sides. After some awkward smiles, a few giggles, and an introduction, they both thought it would be funny to have a picture taken of them together. And so it began.

Charlie stroked one finger over the snuggled-up, laughing couple in the photo.

Choose me, Grace. Please choose me.

3

Grace

The first thing to hit Grace as she stepped over the threshold of Waterside Cottage was the faint scent of cinnamon. She smiled on the inside because it was her favourite smell. Ever since she was a little girl, she loved Christmas, and cinnamon always made an appearance whether in wrapped sticks on the tree, in a mug of hot chocolate, or infused into candles placed around the living room. One Christmas tradition her family had was to put up all the decorations in the morning on the first day of December, without fail. It would appear Waterside Cottage held that tradition too, or at least Hot Doc did.

Grace's eyes lit up as she took in the festive cheer of a home she didn't recognise. She knew Waterside Cottage, as she had passed it by many times whenever she took a trip over to the quaint little place called Pepper Bay. She loved all the cottages along Pepper Lane. Never did she imagine living in one, especially one by Pepper River.

A dark-wood sleeper sat above a large brick fireplace that Charlie was kneeling in front of, lighting some logs. A garland of green leaves entwined with white fairy lights and filled with red berries, red bows, and gold and cream baubles lined the top of the chunky wood. Two tall candles stood either side of the grate upon a black slate surface with holly wrapped around the base of each one.

Grace glanced at the dark wooden beams above her head, lining the white ceiling. A sprig of mistletoe was attached to the one closest to the doorway where she stood, and she noticed Charlie looked her way whilst she was staring at the foliage.

Did he just blush? Was he thinking about kissing me? Nah, I doubt it.

She was glad he turned back to the fire because she was sure she might start blushing.

Scanning the rest of the room, Grace frowned at the lack of a Christmas tree. There were fairy lights lining the French windows on one side of the room and big red bows on the walls either side of the patio doors along the other side. A wicker basket next to a tall vintage lamp held a soft cream blanket, and the rustic coffee table in the middle of the room had the cutest model Christmas village made from wood sitting all along its surface. Inside a tall wooden display cabinet sat three snow globes, all different sizes, and a beautiful old red-and-gold steam train with Christmas presents poking out the tops of its trailers.

Charlie flopped down to the beige tweed rug and crossed his legs. It was obvious he was studying her, but she wasn't sure if it was as her husband or if he was in doctor mode. Either way, she wished he would look somewhere else, as she didn't know how to act. He gestured to the teal sofa when she met his midnight eyes, so she sat upon the edge, tucking her hands under her thighs.

Speak to the man, for crying out loud. It doesn't matter who he is, you can talk to anyone. You've got this.

'I like the Christmas decorations. It looks very festive in here, and cosy.' She removed one hand from beneath her and stroked over the soft furniture. 'This is a lovely colour. The material is nice.' He wasn't joining in the conversation, and his warm smile was making her feel the need to ramble some more. Anything to move her concentration away from his mouth. 'So, erm, I noticed there's no tree. Any reason for that?' She pointed over to a spot by the patio doors, as if that was where a Christmas tree would be placed in the room. She frowned slightly at herself and turned to his gorgeous face, seemingly waiting for her eyes to return to his. Her heart fluttered, causing another frown to cross her face.

'That's something we like to pick out together.'

Grace placed her hand back beneath her thigh as she twisted her mouth to one side. She bobbed her head slightly and she looked away, unable to keep eye contact with him. All she could think of was how crazy the situation was. He was her husband, he's seen her naked, and yet, there she was acting bashful like a girl who had never been alone with a lad before.

Get a grip. You're twenty-nine not nine. Actually, I'm thirty-three, aren't I. Oh flipping heck, this is so weird.

She scanned the room, taking in just how lovely everything looked. It was definitely her cup of tea, from the décor to the Christmas decorations.

'How many trees have we picked together, Dr Wallis... Char... Charlie?'

His chewed bottom lip pinged out from his teeth as a twinkle hit his eyes. He smiled softly, and his eyes fluttered to a close for a moment. 'You helped me pick one for here the first year we met, which was the week after we met, as it was December, and then the year after when you were living here, then the year after that, as soon as we came back from our honeymoon, and then last year. So, I guess that makes four so far.'

'Honeymoon? Oh, so does that mean we're about to have our wedding anniversary then?'

'That would be today. We met on December 1st, and we married on the same date two years later. So, second wedding anniversary, fourth meet-cute anniversary, as Lexi calls it.' He raised his hands to their surroundings. 'I did have more planned for today than this, but, well, you know.'

Grace watched the smile leave his eyes as he glanced down at the rug beneath him. Something about her wanted to go over there and give him the biggest hug, but another part of her said that would be weird, so she remained glued to her awkward sitting position.

Charlie glanced up through those beautiful long lashes she had fast become jealous of. His warmth was back in the room, putting her more at ease. 'Happy anniversary, Gracie.'

What could she say to that? He looked so sad. She figured it was weird for him too.

Ashley's voice entered the living room before she did, which was such a relief for Grace, who was struggling with Charlie and his broken vibe. 'Right, I've put my things in the room next to the bathroom, and I've sorted Grace's hospital bits. I'll put a wash on tomorrow if you like. Might as well make myself useful while I'm here, especially with you working, Charlie.'

'I've taken time off.'

Grace glanced up at her sister hogging the doorway to see her smiling sympathetically at Charlie.

I didn't think about bedrooms. Surely I won't be expected to sleep in the same bed as him.

'Erm...'

Charlie got in first. 'I'll be sleeping in the room next door to you, Grace.'

She was grateful he read her mind. At least he was a gentleman. He had to be a nice man. She wouldn't marry someone she couldn't trust.

I guess Hot Doc won me over. So that makes me Grace Wallis now. Come on, try hard. Try to remember. Something. Anything. Come on. Try.

A pain entered her head, causing the back of her eyes to ache. It must have been noticeable because Charlie was straight by her side. His warm hand covered her brow, soothing every part of her instantly. Before she knew what was happening, she closed her eyes and rested her head upon his cheek, and something about that felt so right until it didn't. She shot up, and the pain in her head made itself known again.

'I'll get you some painkillers, Grace,' said Ashley, fleeing the room as though she were an A&E doctor and not the jewellery maker she was. At least, she was the last Grace knew.

At some point, she would have to speak to her sisters to find out what she'd missed about their lives. Freddy and Molly, for a start. She wondered what else had happened over the last four years, then wondered what the kind doctor was thinking. She couldn't believe she'd almost snuggled into him.

'What's that smile for?' Charlie sat back. His hand was wrapped around her wrist, and she wasn't sure if he was simply holding her or checking her pulse. Either way, it didn't feel strange. In fact, she liked his hand holding her. At least, she thought she did. She pulled away as slowly as possible, as not to cause offence, but a slight shift in his eyes told her the rejection had hurt him.

Ashley returned with painkillers and a glass of water and proceeded to write the time on a Post-it note, which she stuck on top of the cookie shop ornament in the Christmas village. Grace swallowed her pills and went to slouch backwards, but her sister caught her, pulling off her coat. 'Let's make you a bit more comfortable, shall we?'

Charlie disappeared for a moment, and Grace assumed he was hanging up her coat and putting her boots away somewhere. She took a deep breath and smiled gently at her sister.

Ashley sat on a wooden footstool and leaned forward on her elbows. 'How you feeling? You know, you can come home anytime you like. You don't have to stay here. Don't feel obliged or anything. There's no need to be polite about the situation.' She gave a sharp nod. 'Do what's best for you, okay?'

'I said I'd give it a go, and that's what I'll do. I'll be okay. I've only just got here, and honestly, I'm glad to be out of hospital. I wasn't sure how long they were going to keep me in for. It was starting to get boring.' She reached forward and patted Ashley's knee. 'Hey, did you know it's my wedding anniversary today?'

Ashley pulled in her lips as she smiled softly, and Grace sat back and shook her head in disbelief. She glanced at the doorway to see if Charlie was there and was relieved to know he wasn't.

'Ash, I don't remember this place, let alone a wedding.' She pointed at the door and lowered her voice even more. 'Or him. Nothing's coming back, and I tried. I really tried.'

Ashley moved so she was sitting by her sister's side. She reached out and held her hand, lightly stroking her knuckles. 'Hey, hey, don't sweat it. No one expects miracles, even if it is that time of year.' She winked as she breathed out a laugh, and Grace found herself smiling.

But the thought of never being able to remember niggled away. What would happen then? Would she stay with Charlie? Would he want her to? Dr Singh said she mustn't overthink. To take each day as it comes. She needed to focus on her breathing and not let the anniversary business stress her.

'Hey, Grace, how about we get our PJs on early and watch a Christmas film. We love doing that, don't we? We can get some snacks and order Chinese food later. What do you say, you up for that?'

Grace smiled to herself at the memory of slouching in the living room with all her sisters, watching movies and fighting for the last green triangle chocolate in the sweets tin. She could remember so much, just not the last four years. Why was it just that time? Why did it have to be any time?

'You normally like to laze in the bath for an hour before we couch-slouch, Ash. I haven't forgotten that.'

Ashley laughed as she glanced at the door. 'Yeah, but—'

'No buts. If this is my house, then you are more than welcome to go take a long bath. Go on, you get on with that, and I'll put my pyjamas on when you're done. I might have a nose around while you're busy.'

'Are you sure, Grace? I don't like to leave you here alone. Mum would go spare if she found out I left you with Charlie.'

Grace had to laugh. Anyone would think she was a child. 'Ash, he's my husband. I'm pretty sure I married someone decent. Oh goodness, I hope I did. What's he like?'

Ashley shrugged. 'Let's be honest. No one really knows what goes on behind closed doors, but judging by what you say, he's lovely. You've never said a bad word about him. You love him to the moon and back again. We all like him. Mum's only worried because at the moment you don't know him.' She lowered her voice as she leaned closer. 'Grace, you were only with him eight months before you got engaged and moved in here.' She straightened and raised her eyebrows. 'Mind you, that's longer than I waited to move in with my man. Although at first I was just the lodger.'

'Sorry, what? Rewind, Ash. Who are you with?' Much to Grace's frustration, Charlie took that moment to walk back in. She glanced at the large white book he was carrying and then looked at her sister, hoping she would finish her news, but Ashley got up and announced she was off to take a bath.

Charlie placed the book between them on the sofa as he sat down at the other end. 'Are we having a couch and slouch day?'

'I'm sorry. You must have anniversary plans for us. I can tell my sister to—'

'No, Grace. It's fine. Really. We don't need to think about that today. Once you get your memory back, we'll do something then.'

'Will it come back?' She watched him go full-on bedside manner. He was definitely in doctor mode, which only rattled her, as she figured her husband would be more truthful than a doctor. Dr Wallis was being the doctor who wouldn't commit to an answer in case he got it wrong and got sued for his trouble.

That warm smile she had already got used to made an appearance. 'I'm optimistic,' he said softly. And that's all she got about that. He tapped the book and the twinkle in his eyes returned.

He's like Christmas when that twinkle appears. He could be from the North Pole, for all I know. One of Santa's helpers. I'm not afraid of you, stranger.

'This is our wedding book. We've got most of our pictures on the computer, but you wanted some printed out for this book you bought online. I thought you might like a peek. It could help settle you around me, if nothing else. My proof that I am who I say I am.' He breathed out a laugh, and she smiled down at the wording on the front cover.

'Mr & Mrs Wallis.' She pulled the book to her lap and turned the page to see the first picture. A 5x8 colour photograph of herself in an off-the-shoulder wedding dress made from cream satin and lace. Her highlighted blonde hair was pulled up from her shoulders and twisted and curled at the back of her head, with dainty gyp threaded throughout. Her bouquet was white roses and freesias tied with a cream ribbon. 'Oh, I look—'

'Incredible.'

Grace loosened the grip she had on the book and blinked away the tears threatening to fall. She carefully turned the page to see Charlie wearing a dark wedding suit with a cream cravat and a white rose in his lapel. He was standing by a long, ornate window, looking out at a snow-covered garden. 'Wow, Charlie, you look—'

'Enchanting?'

She giggled and looked up to meet his smiling eyes and friendly face. 'Where is this place?'

'Canada. It's where I'm from. You wanted to get married there, so we all went.' He narrowed his eyes and grinned. 'You thought I was American, didn't you? You did the first time you heard me speak.'

Grace didn't answer, she was too busy feeling excited about the fact she went to Canada, then disappointed she couldn't remember the trip. She turned the page to see one of them together in the snow. 'How long did we stay out there?'

'We went out in November, got married the first day of December, so three weeks in total, then everyone went home and we went on our honeymoon.'

Grace's head jolted up. 'Oh, I don't remember.' She looked back sadly at the photograph. 'I'm sorry. I wish I could remember this day, if nothing else. It was obviously very special.'

He dipped his head and looked up through his lashes. 'Yes, it was.' He shuffled in his seat, appearing nervous about something. 'Look, Grace. I really want you to remember me. I miss you so much already. It's hard not being able to hold you whenever I want, but I understand, better than most, what's happened to you. So, what I'm asking for is for you to just give me a chance. Christmas is our time. It's when we met, when we fell in love, when we got married. It just means a lot to us both. What I mean to say is, whatever happens, will you just stick around? Stay here this Christmas, with me. Let me remind you of the Christmas you fell in love with me. I want to take you back to Christmas past.'

A small laugh escaped Grace's mouth. 'You make me sound like Scrooge.'

Charlie's warm smile was back. 'Sorry, that came out wrong, but you know where I'm coming from, right?' She nodded. 'So, will you give me a shot at this? You never know, you might actually like me.'

Grace took another look at the wedding photo of them both. The couple in the picture looked very much in love. She just wished she could feel the emotion she was seeing.

She guessed she didn't have anything to lose. It was just Christmas, and if by the end of the season she still didn't remember him, or fall madly in love with him, she could go back home.

Why does that thought sadden me? I always liked living at home.

She glanced around the living room at the fire crackling away, the Christmas cheer thrown everywhere, and some of the ornaments she knew were hers from back home, like the red-and-gold Nutcracker standing proudly by the back doors. 'Okay, Charlie. I'm yours for Christmas.'

His smile could have lit the whole island, and in turn made her smile shyly back. 'So, Gracie, when you say that you're mine, does that mean…' He waggled his eyebrows playfully.

'Hey, don't push your luck.' She liked his laugh, and how it made her feel instantly happy. 'I have a condition about this Christmas malarkey though.'

He showed his palms and lowered his head submissively. 'Anything you want. You name it, it's done.'

Grace pointed over to the empty corner by the patio doors. 'First thing tomorrow, we buy a Christmas tree.'

'Ooh, great choice. Frozen Forest, here we come.'

Grace frowned with amusement. 'Frozen Forest? Is that a place? I take it it's new, so where is it? Still on the island?'

He shushed her by leaning closer and placing his fingertips lightly over her lips, causing a flutter to hit her chest, much to her surprise. 'Too many questions.' He lowered his hand, looking embarrassed about what he had done. 'Let me just date you, okay? And that means I get to take you out and surprise you. Trust me, you're gonna love this Christmas.' His smile faltered a touch, and he swallowed hard. 'You can bring Ashley too, if you want.'

'Well, that's nice of you, but I've never brought one of my sisters on a date before, so I don't think I should start now.' She watched him smile and reach out to her hand and then pull back, obviously thinking better of it. 'Can I just say, please don't expect too much from me, will you? I know I'm your wife, but I don't know you. I don't feel ready to kiss you or anything.'

'Hey, Grace, I'm not expecting anything from you. There won't be any pressure from me. You can count on that.' He gestured to the mistletoe. 'You want me to remove that?'

She glanced over her shoulder and laughed to herself. 'Nah, it's okay. I'm sure we can ignore it if we happen to bump into each other beneath its almighty powers.'

Charlie grinned. 'You know, it's you who always grabs me whenever there's mistletoe hanging around.' He pointed to his lips. 'You can't get enough of these bad boys.'

Grace felt the pull on her stomach as she laughed out loud for the first time since waking from her coma. 'I won't lie, you do have a very kissable mouth, Dr Wallis.'

'Thank you, Mrs Wallis. It's here whenever you want it. Seriously, you don't even have to ask.'

Grace knew she was blushing, as she could feel the heat in her face. 'We'll see.'

Charlie gave her a cheeky wink. 'Yep. We'll see.'

4

Charlie

Charlie watched Grace's eyes light up as she peered out the side window of his car. He slowed his yellow beetle so she could enjoy the rows of Christmas trees along the driveway of Silver Wish Farm. They had bought their tree from there every year, but it was only the year before that the owners created the Frozen Forest as a new attraction to their garden centre. It was only a matter of time before Grace asked the question he knew was whirling in her head.

'This is Silver Wish Farm. There's no Frozen Forest here.' She turned his way. 'Is there, Charlie?'

'It's a new thing they're doing at Christmas. We went to the opening day last year. It's really nice what they've done. You're gonna love it, trust me.'

'I'm definitely intrigued.'

'That's a good start.' He glanced at the dash to see whose name was flashing up on his phone. 'It's your mum. Again. You wanna get that?'

'No. I'll send her a quick text when we park. I already told her you were taking me out today. She keeps fussing. I'm really not keen on being treated like a child. I hope you won't do the same.'

'I won't. I promise. However, you haven't been out of hospital long, so we're gonna take things slowly, okay? We won't be doing the whole day when we're out. Just a few hours a day, and just one thing every other day or every few days should be fine. You'll need rest days in between.'

Grace huffed and rolled her eyes. 'Hey, I did all my exercises. I'm not as weak as I was. My physiotherapist was happy with my progress. Plus, I'm still working my muscles each morning. I think I can cope with being out all day.'

'I'm sure you can, but you're under doctor's orders to take it easy for a while, so those are the rules, Grace.'

'Which doctor said that?'

Charlie tapped his chest and grinned. 'This one.' His smile stretched even wider when she snorted out a laugh whilst nudging his arm. Just the fact she felt comfortable enough to play-nudge him made him feel hopeful for their future.

A hand-painted sign attached to a large candy cane, which looked best suited to Lapland, pointed the way to the car park. They pulled up and Grace sent her mum a text before they stepped out onto the dry field where only a handful of cars had parked.

'It's a shame we missed the Sandly Christmas Market yesterday.' Grace smiled softly at him, but he could see she felt as though it were her fault he had missed out on the opportunity to celebrate their wedding anniversary somewhere they met.

He flapped one hand her way. 'Ah, we'll catch up with it next year. Meanwhile, this year has a lot more to offer.'

Grace seemed to relax a little. 'Not sure how much. This is the Isle of Wight, you know, not Norway.'

'Oh, you'd be surprised how Christmassy this place can be.'

'Well, not really. I've lived here all my life. I haven't forgotten that much.'

Charlie walked around the car to stand at her side. He placed his hands in his coat pockets and offered out his elbow, hoping she would hold on to his arm. She was considering it, that much was clear. 'You just have to look around you, Grace. Christmas is so magical, it can pop up anywhere. But don't worry, I'm going to show you. All you have to do is follow me.'

Grace linked arms with him, which filled his heart. He warmed at the bashful look in her eyes and the hint of pink that hit her cheeks. It wasn't something he had witnessed about her for a long while. He found it kind of cute that the woman he met four years ago was making an appearance.

He wished she could remember everything, but starting over with her was bringing back a lot of memories for him, which was nice. It seemed wrong to be enjoying the moment. Although, after what had happened, he figured he should enjoy every moment, old or new.

Okay, let's do this. Let's see if the Christmas present can bring back the Christmas past for Grace.

Charlie gestured towards a white marquee that had a large reindeer on either side of the entrance and a sign above the doorway letting them know they were about to enter the Frozen Forest. He gave Grace's arm a gentle squeeze as they stepped inside to buy their tickets.

A young man dressed as a postmaster in a blue-and-silver costume greeted them with a big friendly smile. His cheeks held perfectly round red blobs of makeup, and there was a glittery shine to his forehead and chin. The sparkly silver tassels on his cuffs shimmered when his hand stretched out to exchange money for two white admission cards. 'Hey, Grace. Good to see you up and about.'

Grace leaned closer, examining the man's face. 'Tyler Silver, is that you?' She laughed as she poked his shiny *Postie* badge. 'What has your dad got you doing now?'

Tyler tipped his blue hat as he bowed. 'It's not my dad, it's Santa. We all have to pull our weight this time of year.

Therefore, I am not Tyler Silver of Silver Wish Farm. I am the North Pole Postmaster. Also known as the Gatekeeper of the Frozen Forest.' He waggled out one hand, rolling it around, then pointed to another canvas doorway. 'Step inside and stay on the pathway. You don't want to attract any wolves.' He wiggled his fingers at Charlie and winked at Grace. 'And please don't feed the reindeers. They're really not partial to cheese and onion crisps.'

Grace giggled and snuggled further into Charlie's side as they entered the second part of the large tent.

Oh, Grace, if only I could kiss you right now.

He had to keep reminding himself it was their first date. Holding his arm was good enough. Not every first date had that included. She was feeling okay with him. He was sure. Now he just had to see if the winter wonderland sparked anything.

'Ooh, Charlie, look at this place. It's beautiful.' Grace's eyes sparkled in the blue and white lighting of the large icy area, and Charlie's smile reached every part of him.

The blue pathway beneath their boots directed them along ice sculptures of woodland creatures and small pine trees that filled the air with the hint of their balsam scent. Twinkling white fairy lights lined the edges of the snowy scenes, and silver stars of all sizes hung from the roof.

Charlie gathered Grace in front of him and adjusted her cream scarf. 'You warm enough, honey? It's cold in here.' He tugged her woolly hat further over her ears and flashed his best smile.

'I'm okay, thanks. I'm well wrapped up. We both are. No fussing, okay?' She lowered his hand from her hair, and that's when he realised he was playing with the tips of her loose locks. He offered his arm again, and they walked further along to see the wolves Tyler had mentioned.

A pack of grey-and-white, large and small, animatronic wolves moved their heads slowly from side to side and up and down. The largest was sniffing a tree, and the youngest cub kept resting its head against its mother.

'They look kind of real.' Grace let go of his arm to lean closer for a better look, and Charlie pulled out his phone and took a picture. She turned and beamed a smile his way, so he took another.

'You know, you're normally the photographer.'

Grace shrugged one shoulder as she cooed over the fluffy cub. 'Photography is just something I dabble with, that's all. I don't mind you being in charge of that today. Take one of the wolves.'

Charlie stepped to her side as she straightened. 'It's more than a hobby for you now. We were going to set up the extension as your studio next year. Somewhere for your clients to go.'

'Clients? I don't have any clients.'

He nodded and pulled up her Instagram account on his phone. 'You're currently working on your website that should be up and running in the new year, but you've got this account at the moment. See this picture here, that's the first school shoot you got asked to do. And look...' He came off Instagram to show her his photo album. Her eyes were studying the headshot of his hospital pass. 'You took that. That was our second meeting. You got the contract to take the mugshots for all the hospital staff. We have to renew our pictures every so often. That's when I asked you out.'

Grace met his eyes and smiled with confusion. 'Our second meeting? You mean nothing happened the first time we met?'

'Oh, something happened. To me, at least. You had my heart all a flutter.' He dramatically slapped his hands to his chest and dropped his head whilst batting his eyelashes up at her. Grace laughed as he straightened. 'But I was too much of a coward to ask you out then, and trust me when I tell you, I spent the whole night awake regretting that. I was so happy to see you two days later in the hospital when I walked in to have my picture taken. Not gonna lie, I thanked the universe.'

There was something about Grace's laugh that always warmed him. It had a huskiness to it that made her sound sexy as hell.

Grace moved down the pathway towards a cluster of snow-covered Nordmann fir trees. 'Did you know the Silver family get a lot of their trees from a farm up in Scotland? It's in the Scottish Highlands. A place called Emerald Tree Farm in Honeydale. The Silvers don't have enough land to grow as many as they'd like. Plus, their trees are quite small here. The owner, Benton Silver, told me that once. See, I remember a lot.' She flashed a cheesy grin and turned to admire the adorable penguins ice-skating on a round mirror. 'They have a furniture shop here too. The eldest son, Heath, can pretty much make anything out of a lump of wood. Did you see Santa's sleigh up by their house when we drove in? Not that you can miss it. It's huge. Heath made that years ago.'

Cold air escaped Charlie's lips as he parted them to breathe out a quiet laugh. 'You don't have to convince me of your memory skills, Grace.'

She sighed deeply, lowering her shoulders whilst stepping closer to him. 'Yeah, I know. I just wish I could remember more recent stuff.'

He placed his hands on her shoulders and pulled her into his chest for a cuddle. 'I know, honey. It'll come back.' He moved her away slightly so he could see her face. 'Don't try so hard, okay?'

Oh crap, I just hugged her by habit. Not sure how that went down. I'm a stranger to her, after all. I need to stay focused here. I can't scare her away.

He dropped his hands and lowered his head, raising his eyes at her. 'Sorry about that. I'm the one who forgot myself there.' He loved the bashful smile that kept making an appearance on her face. It was beyond adorable. He moved out of her personal space and gestured over at the penguins. 'Got to love a penguin. I do believe some of them mate for life.'

And I said that why?

Grace turned to stare at the icy scene. 'Unless the other penguin doesn't return home. Then they carry on with someone else.'

Is she trying to tell me something there? I'm overthinking this. We're just talking penguins. Let's move on.

Charlie walked through a short tunnel filled with hanging silver strips of shiny foil where fake snow lightly fell. He reached out one hand and was pleased to feel Grace's gloved fingers slip between his. Pulling her into the passageway, he started to sing 'Let it Snow'. Much to his delight, she quietly joined in. Just like she used to.

5

Grace

It was the small bags of peppermint bark that Grace headed straight towards in the shop at the other end of the Frozen Forest. She picked up three bags, as she wanted one for Ashley as well. She glanced over her shoulder to see Charlie paying for the photo the camera in the snowflake tunnel had taken of them. She could see from where she was it was a beautiful picture of them both laughing at the end of the song they had sung.

I hope I don't forget this day.

She fumbled with some wooden trinkets of small foxes and hedgehogs loose in a big blue ceramic bowl. They reminded her of the type of jewellery Ashley would make to sell in her online shop. She made a mental note to find out if Ashley was still doing that. There was so much she might be unaware of. A catch-up with her sisters was definitely on the cards.

The warmth of Charlie's body crept through her wool-blend grey coat. There was something calming about his close proximity that was starting to fascinate her. She turned and showed him the goods she wanted to buy, and he produced a soft, cuddly penguin.

'This is for you, Grace. His name is Charlie, and if his mate never returns home, he will not just carry on.' He lightly tapped her nose with its head, then swapped the toy for the peppermint bark.

Grace stared down at the fluffy penguin whilst Charlie went back to the till.

Oh, Hot Doc is really sweet. I can see why past me liked him. Do I still like him? He is nice, but it's early days.

She was still confused. And so tired all of a sudden. She wasn't sure if she should mention that. They hadn't bought their tree yet. She decided not to say anything, as they were about to head outside anyway so wouldn't be much longer.

She snuggled Penguin Charlie into her nose for a second before picking up a peppermint-infused candle and heading over to the till.

Charlie paid for everything, explaining it was money from their joint account. But Grace secretly suspected he was using the card from his own account. It seemed like the type of thing he would do. She was just unsure why she would think that about him.

'Come on, Grace, let's go pick a tree.'

Afternoon had shifted to evening, but it didn't matter where the trees were for sale, as multicoloured lights lit up the whole area. The smell of freshly cut wood filled the cool air, and Christmas music wafted from nearby speakers, which made them laugh when a crackle was heard followed by a scratching noise and then silence.

Tyler sprinted out through the trees to pass them, making Grace jump back and fall into Charlie, who caught her with both hands and held her close.

Tyler tapped the top of his hat. 'Sorry about that. One sec.'

Grace straightened and thanked Charlie for his quick reflexes.

'Hey, I work in A&E. All my skills are quick.' He frowned with annoyance and shook his head. 'That's not entirely true. I mean, I know how to slow down too. Take my time. I don't rush our…'

Grace tried hard not to giggle at him fumbling over his words and the serious expression on his face. His cheeks had reddened a touch and he seemed somewhat flustered.

Charlie raked his hand under his blue woolly hat, causing it to rise up his head. 'Okay, so I'm just gonna stop talking. Hey, look, this is a nice tree.'

She stood at his side and slowly nudged his arm with her shoulder. 'Good to know about your skills, Charlie.'

He groaned, making her snort out the laugh she had tried so desperately hard to hold in.

Grace moved along the trees, feeling fatigue creep into her body. She brushed her hand over some branches and sniffed her gloves, enjoying the woodland smell. 'I like this one. Is five foot okay with you?' She steadied herself by leaning back onto Charlie as soon as he approached. Closing her eyes for a moment, she took a breath and hoped he hadn't noticed any change in her.

Charlie reached over her to fiddle with a branch. 'Yeah, that's what we normally get.' He settled his hand on her shoulder, then his head to the side of her face. 'Let's get this and head home now.' He steered her around and gestured to a wooden bench just behind them. 'You wait here while I go get Tyler to net this tree.'

Grace allowed him to guide her onto the seat, as she was happy to sit down for a bit. She figured her energy would return any minute. Her physiotherapist had warned her it would take some time to get back to normal. She accepted the information but didn't expect to feel so whacked-out as often as she did since she left the hospital. Her mind drifted back to the first time she had to get out of bed after waking from a coma.

Jelly legs. More like no legs.

She was worried back then, so was her mum. She was so grateful when she walked, thinking for a moment it wasn't going to happen, as her muscles were that weak.

Looking down at her legs, her mind whirled. What if she stayed weak forever? Would she need a wheelchair one day? She wondered if she would ever fully recover.

Trying to take her mind off her weary body, Grace glanced over to the trees to see an older couple mooching through the mini forest the cluster had made. She smiled at the elderly couple's entwined hands and the smile on their faces that looked warm and content.

I hope I grow old with someone I love and who loves me just as much.

She focused on the Christmas music filling the air, but it was difficult to concentrate on her surroundings, as thoughts of Ashley telling her about the hit and run appeared.

A flashback filled her mind of a streetlight and the noise of screeching tyres, then it was gone. Lowering her head and covering her eyes with her hand as though trying to block out a bright light made her feel worse. She jumped and jolted upright, seeing only the elderly couple in amongst the trees again.

Ashley's words echoed around her. 'Viktor Blake paid him to hurt you just to get at me because he was jealous. They got him, Grace. They got them both. Don't you worry about that. They're banged up now, and bail was refused. Good bloody job too. If I ever get my hands on them, I'll…'

The Christmas music seemed louder, causing Grace to look up at the speaker to hear 'Jingle Bells' belting out. Her heart rate seemed to be bouncing along to the beat, so she took some calming breaths to help settle herself. She didn't want to feel anxious. Christmas was her favourite time of year, and she was having a lovely day with Charlie.

She reached into the cloth shopping bag that Charlie had placed by her feet and rummaged around until she found the peppermint bark. She pulled off her gloves and unwrapped the cellophane and snapped off a piece of chocolate. The smell and taste of peppermint made her smile as she popped the candy into her mouth.

'Mmm. Now, this is what the doctor ordered.' She giggled to herself, then ate another piece. 'A peppermint hot chocolate wouldn't go amiss. I wonder if the Gatehouse Café still exists.'

'It does,' said a large muscular man, plonking himself down to her side. His dark-brown eyes peered into hers. 'Do you know who I am?'

Grace scrunched her nose, tilted her head, and tightened her eyes. 'Your name is Heath Silver. Does that help you?'

Heath roared out a throaty laugh. 'I don't know how much you remember.'

'I remember you, Heath. Blooming heck! It's just the last four years I'm having trouble with, that's all, which does mean you look older.'

Heath grinned whilst nodding. 'Yep, sounds about right. I think I age ten years every year.' He pointed to the corner of his right eye. 'See. Lines.'

Grace pointed beneath her eyes. 'Beats dark circles. I look like I've been boxing.'

'You look good, Grace.' His deep voice softened. 'How are you doing now? It's good to see you up and about.'

'I'm getting there. How are things with you, Heath? Any changes I've forgotten about?' She poked his red plaid jacket. 'Still rocking the lumberjack look, I see.'

He breathed out cold air as he glanced down at his thick coat. 'I like this look.'

'Are you still fighting with Rhett Smithson about the gate dividing your land?' She nudged his arm playfully, making his grin widen.

'That's what you want to remember?'

Grace tapped her temple. 'Hey, this thing's playing by its own rules at the moment.'

Heath crossed his arms in front of his solid chest. 'We don't fight over the gate. Well, there was one time... Anyway, I'm not talking about her. Actually, I'm not talking to her at the moment.'

'Oh, I always thought you two would end up together.'

'Really? Why?'

Grace shrugged. 'Well, there's the fact you have a daughter together. I would've thought she might have brought you two back to each other.'

Heath flapped one hand. 'Ah, we've practically ignored each other since our Willow was born.'

'Our Lexi would call it enemies to lovers. She loves all the tropes, but that's her favourite. She's always reading romance books or watching lovey-dovey films.'

Heath nodded as he turned so he was facing her full on. 'Yeah, her books are doing really well, I hear.'

'What books?'

'Her own ones. The ones she writes. I guess no one has caught you up on that snippet of info yet.'

Grace shook her head. 'Nope. I really do need a catch-up with my sisters. So, Lexi's an author. Makes sense. Ooh, did you know that my little sister Kerri had a baby this year? That was a surprise. Even more so seeing our Lexi about to give birth any day now, and I still haven't been told who her partner is. People keep drip-feeding me bits and bobs, which is quite annoying. I want to know everything all at once.' She breathed out a laugh whilst shaking her head at herself. 'I guess I still lack patience.'

'Well, I can tell you something about Lexi's partner, if you want?'

'Ooh, yes, spill the beans. I'm completely open to any gossip you have to offer.' She handed him a piece of peppermint bark and snuggled down into her scarf, ready to hear something juicy, she hoped.

He took a bite, chewed, swallowed, and seemed to be tormenting her by stalling until she slapped his thigh. 'Okay, okay. Well, Lexi is with my cousin, Bryce.'

Grace's eyes widened as far as they could go. 'Flipping heck. Of all people. She ends up with Not-Nice-Bryce. Well, now there's a turn up for the books.'

Heath laughed, almost spitting out his bite of peppermint bark. 'Not-Nice-Bryce? Is that what you call him?'

'Lexi used to call him that when she was a kid. Well, they were always at odds with each other. See. Enemies to lovers, right there.' She playfully nudged his arm. 'Could be you and Rhett next.' Heath went to answer but was interrupted by Charlie's return with Tyler. Grace watched her husband pointing out the tree they wanted.

Tyler gestured to his big brother to help, and Heath picked up the tree by himself, leaving Tyler to guide the buyers over to a payment hut lined with green garlands embedded with twinkling lights.

Grace leaned into Charlie's side as their chosen tree was netted and carried out to their car. 'Hey, there's a café up the road. Do you fancy a peppermint hot chocolate over there?'

Charlie smiled warmly. 'Sure. Come on, let's get you in the car. You can switch the heating on while we strap the tree to the roof.'

'Sounds like a good plan to me.' She took his arm and tried hard not to slouch her way to the car park. She was sure he could tell she was flaking.

The warmth inside the vehicle was welcome, and she removed her scarf and gloves, placing her cold fingers in front of the hot air vent. Outside, Charlie was helping Heath secure the tree to the roof whilst Tyler went back to the Frozen Forest.

Grace felt a wave of happiness flood her. It didn't matter that the evening was cold and dark, or she was sitting in a car park. Even the thudding noise on the roof wasn't bothering her mood. She was content, and the relaxed feeling made every part of her smile. She couldn't quite put her finger on it, but there was definitely something familiar about the cosiness of her present situation.

She heard muffled voices and saw Heath wave to her as the driver's door opened and Charlie climbed in. He had a big soppy grin across his face that instantly made her smile. 'What are you grinning about?'

'The tree fell off on our way home last year.'

'Oh, goodness, that's all we need.'

He gave a slight nod and lost some of his smile. 'You good to go?'

'Yep. I'm looking forward to my peppermint hot chocolate. And, Charlie, thanks for today. It's been really nice.'

Charlie flashed that smile her heart seemed to like, and something else suddenly felt familiar, though she wasn't sure what.

6

Charlie

The Gatehouse Café was a large, two-story, log cabin with a dark roof that looked slightly lost on the borderline of two farms, and much better suited to the snowy Alps of Switzerland.

'Do you know the story of this place, Charlie?' Before he had a chance to answer, Grace carried on. 'It was built by Heath and Tyler's great-grandfather, Neville Silver. He fell in love with Abbigail Smithson, the daughter of the owner of the joining land, and the story goes, she promised to marry him if he built her a new home. He did. She took ownership of the building, then refused to marry him. There was a big fight between her brother and Neville, and that was the end of that. So, you see, the Gatehouse Café might belong to the Smithson family, but it's on Silver Wish Farm.'

The car pulled up in a small gravel car park alongside a thick wooden, rotted old gate.

'That's why it's called the Gatehouse.' Grace pointed over at the divide. 'That gate is the border for Silver Wish Farm and Lucky Riding Stables. Apparently, Neville was so mad, he built the gate and told the Smithsons never to cross it or else. He then went on to build a dividing fence. Scandal, eh, Charlie?'

'You don't have to keep giving me history lessons to prove your memory still works, Grace.'

'I wasn't. It's a good story.'

He glanced up at the old cabin lined with multicoloured Christmas lights and fake icicles hanging from the guttering.

'Yeah, it's a good story. Unless you're a Silver. They might not find it amusing. I wonder what they think about this place being on their land?'

Grace shrugged as she got out of the car. 'Don't know. They've never done anything about it. I don't think they're too bothered. I'm still waiting for Heath and Rhett to get together. They hate each other, or so it seems. After Lexi and Bryce, who knows what might happen. Did you know Rhett's mum was a massive fan of the film *Gone with the Wind*, and that's why she named her daughters Rhett and Vivien?'

A smile tugged at Charlie's mouth. 'Yeah, I know that story too.'

Warm air and freshly roasted coffee hit Charlie as soon as he opened the door to the café for Grace to enter. He smiled at the tiny Christmas trees sitting upon each square table and pulled out a chair by the window for Grace so she would have a view of the small duck pond by the outside seating area.

He went to the counter and ordered two large peppermint hot chocolates, then joined Grace at the table.

'I love it in here, Charlie. It's always so cosy, no matter what the season.'

'Yeah, not many cafés have a real fire.' He glanced over at the old brick fireplace lined with red candles and six reindeers pulling a sleigh, then turned back her way. 'You warm enough?'

Grace had already removed her coat and was tucking her gloves away into the pockets. 'Yeah, I'm good. We'll have this, then go home and decorate our tree. That could be a new tradition. We buy the tree, come in here for a hot chocolate, then go home and decorate before dinner.'

Charlie felt the smile in his heart appear before the one on his face. 'That's what we've been doing, Grace.' It warmed him to see her smile.

'Do you think I remembered that without remembering?'

'I guess it just felt natural to you. That's a good sign.' He wanted to say more but was interrupted by a lady bringing over their drinks. Her long dark ponytail swished behind her as she bent over to kiss Grace on the cheek.

'So glad to see you, chick.' She straightened and pointed at herself. 'I was going to come to the hospital when I heard you woke up, but I knew your whole family would be there, so I was hoping to pop in and see you sometime this week. Guess I don't need to now. Wait. You do remember me, right?'

Grace breathed out a laugh. 'Why does everyone keep asking me that? It's only the last four years I can't remember, Vivien.'

Charlie tapped his chest. 'I'm the only stranger.' A fizz of excitement lodged in his heart when Grace's hand slid across the table to gently pat his.

Vivien smiled warmly at them both. 'Well, I guess that is kind of strange for you, Charlie. But never mind, Grace, you will just fall in love with him all over again instead.' She winked at Grace as she nudged her shoulder. 'I mean, come on, what's not to like about this fella? Hot Doc alert. And he has a super-sexy accent.'

Charlie gave a slight bow as he laughed. 'Why thank you, Viv.'

'Credit where credit's due, I say. Shame there aren't more like you around here.'

Grace frowned as her lips twisted to one side. 'Hmm, I wouldn't let Brody hear you say that, Viv. I'm not sure your partner will be best pleased.' She gestured behind her. 'Or Finn. You'll break his heart.'

Vivien flapped her hand behind her to the far corner of the room where a tall, athletic-built man sat writing in a notebook. 'We're just friends. You know that, so no teasing him.'

Charlie glanced over at Finn Silver. 'He looks like a slimmer version of Heath, don't you think?'

Finn took that moment to look up as though he knew he was being spoken about. Grace blew him a kiss as he waved her way. 'You okay, Grace?'

'I'm doing fine, thanks, Finn. I just want everyone around me to act normal.'

Finn gave her the thumbs-up and glanced at Vivien.

Vivien flashed him a smile, and he went back to his book.

'Finn's always been lovely. And he's your best friend. Excluding me, that is.' Grace smiled at Charlie. 'So, go and sit with him, that way you'll stop ogling my man.'

Vivien bent to smooch Charlie's cold cheeks. 'Ooh, but he's lovely, Grace. He deserves the odd ogle.'

Charlie laughed whilst removing his face from her grip. 'Get off me, woman. I want to eat my cookie snowman.' He gestured to the small biscuit resting on top of a swirl of whipped cream upon his hot chocolate.

'Okay, I will leave you lovebirds alone. Just shout if you need anything. And, Grace, we'll have a proper catch-up soon.' Vivien clamped her hands over her heart as water filled her dark eyes. 'I really missed my bestie, you know. Love you, chick.'

'Love you too, Viv.' Grace beamed into her large glass as her friend went back to work. 'Ooh, this looks too good to touch.' She put her snowman on a saucer and swirled a candy cane around the cream, mixing in the red crystal sprinkles scattered on top.

Charlie copied her actions whilst grinning to himself.

She called me her man. I guess she's warming to me. I think she likes me. Oh great, I'm right back where I started.

He could remember thinking that way when they first met. He was pretty dumb around her back then. At least he wasn't making a complete idiot of himself this time. He hoped.

Grace leaned closer across the table, beckoning him towards her. 'She's still with Brody, isn't she?' she whispered, looking sideways to make sure her friend wasn't about. 'She didn't actually say.'

He pulled in his lips and gave a sympathetic smile. 'Yeah, sorry. I know you don't like him.'

'Is he still in the police force?'

'Yep.'

She sat back and sighed. 'Oh dear.' Another sigh later and a sip of her drink, and Grace seemed to look relaxed again. Only, she'd been quiet for a while, which rattled him a touch.

He wanted to know what she was thinking about. Her friend? Him? Her life? He wished he could fix her head.

'Charlie, tell me about yourself. I know you come from Canada, obviously, but I don't know much else.'

'Erm, okay, well, I'm thirty-seven. I'm the middle child of three. There's my older brother, William, and my younger sister, Amy. They still live in Canada. My parents are both doctors too. Peter and Charlene. I went to medical school back home, then came to England to study, then I worked in a hospital in London for a while before coming here.'

'Wow, your life sounds so interesting. I've only ever worked at the Donkey Sanctuary.'

'And now you're a photographer too.'

She shrugged and smiled softly. 'Yeah, I guess.'

He wasn't keen on how sad she sounded about that fact. Sure, he knew she couldn't remember the career she was slowly building for herself, but he wanted her to feel as proud about herself as he did. 'You know, working with those donkeys is so fulfilling for you. You really make a difference, Grace. Even with the photography studio we were planning for you, you weren't going to turn your back on the sanctuary. You wanted to work both part time.'

'I do love it there.'

'Yeah, you do. And what's not to love about donkeys. Sometimes I'd like to be a vet. Working with animals has got to be better than some of the rowdy humans I have to deal with at times.'

Grace laughed into her hot drink. 'Oh, you love your job.' Her blue eyes flew his way in surprise. 'I think. I don't know why I assumed that.'

The corners of his eyes creased, he was smiling that much. 'You didn't assume. You knew.' He reached forward and held her hand on the table. 'Grace, I truly believe that every memory we've made together is right there in your mind, tucked away somewhere safe just waiting to make an appearance. And they will. Soon.'

Grace slowly pulled her hand back, using it to pick up her snowman cookie, but Charlie felt a touch deflated that she hadn't wanted to stay touching hands.

He needed to slow down. Stop trying to touch her all the time. She wasn't used to him, and he had to remind himself of that. It was difficult, but at least she was giving him a chance. But that was his Grace. If she tried something, she went all in.

He sipped his drink, inhaling the peppermint aroma, whilst watching Grace as she hummed along to 'Frosty the

Snowman' playing on the radio. If he didn't know any better, he would have thought everything was perfectly normal.

His life had changed dramatically, and his wife's condition was weighing heavily on his shoulders, but he couldn't fall. She needed him to be strong. No matter how run-down he was feeling, he had to plaster on that doctor smile he had perfected years ago and get on with the task at hand.

Only, this time, it wasn't a task, nor his job. This was his wife. The woman who held his heart. And there wasn't anything he could do to fix her. All he could do was be there and hope that, one day, she would remember him. Remember them.

7

Grace

The box Charlie brought down from the loft contained large ornate baubles, green and gold ribbons, and hand-carved wooden ornaments.

Grace picked out a wooden gingerbread man and placed it close to the bottom of the Christmas tree where she sat. 'These are gorgeous. So well made. I take it we bought these up at Silver Wish Farm?' She held up a wooden star. 'They just scream Heath Silver.'

'Yeah, we bought those there, and the glass baubles at Sandly Christmas Market. Your mum gave us the ribbons, not sure where she got those, and we bought some bits online. That ceramic reindeer was made by Ashley. I think it was supposed to go on a necklace, but the ear chipped, and you wouldn't let her throw it away, so it now has a home with us.'

She took the reindeer from him and placed it on the tree. 'Do they still bring reindeers to the zoo for Christmas? I'd like to go see them if they do.'

Charlie manoeuvred around the other side of the tree to tuck in some gold ribbon. 'Yeah, we went the year we got married. We only had a week before Christmas to pack everything in that year, because we went straight on our honeymoon from Canada, and by the time we got home, it was six days to Christmas. We did a lot though.'

She peered around the tree to see him smiling to himself at the memories only he could see. 'Where did we go for our honeymoon?' The beam of a smile that flashed her way caused her stomach to flip.

Goodness, Charlie. Do you have any idea how great your smile is? You have such nice eyes as well. Ones filled with dreams.

'We went to Lapland.'

She slapped her hands down to the rug beneath her. 'No way!'

'Way.'

'I've always wanted to go there. I want to see the Northern Lights. Oh, I missed it.' Her wide eyes narrowed as her shoulders slumped and her smile faded. 'I can't believe I don't remember.'

'You'll see them again, Gracie. That's a promise.'

She gazed up at him, wanting to know all about their Christmas adventure. He sat and leaned back against the wall next to the fireplace. Grace could already feel the warmth from the crackling logs, but having Charlie sitting opposite her looking dreamy was warming her even more.

'What was it like there, Charlie?' She cleared her throat, as she heard her words crack as she spoke. She didn't want him to know just how sad she was about not remembering their honeymoon. Lapland, of all places. They went there. Her dream place, and she couldn't remember.

'We left the airport and travelled to our hotel by snow ski. Yep, that was an experience. Our bedroom was a glass igloo in among snowy woodland, which you fell completely in love with. Way more than you love me. There was a log cabin attached, where we had a jacuzzi bathtub and kitchenette. It was warm, cosy, and we didn't want to leave. We went to a snow village and had dinner in an ice restaurant, and we took a trip on a husky sled, and come nightfall, it was like we were in space itself, there were that many stars to see. And, yes, we saw the Northern Lights.'

Grace closed her eyes, trying desperately to remember something. Anything. Just the thought had her smiling from ear to ear, so she knew what actually being there would do to her. Charlie's soft voice wrapped around her like a comfort blanket, snuggling her further and further into dreamland.

'We went swimming one night over in the warm glow of the pool in the main lodge and ate creamy chocolate on our way back home. The snow was deep and crunchy beneath our boots, and the air was fresh and icy. Fairy lights made the pathways, and the snowman we had made that morning helped us find which igloo was ours. We drank champagne in the bath, put on matching fleece pyjamas, and sat up in bed watching the sky.'

Is he going to mention any love-making that probably took place? He can see it, can't he? Feeling everything we experienced.

Grace opened her eyes in time to see a lone teardrop leak from Charlie's eye and roll down over his cheekbone. He quickly swiped it away and sniffed, and she offered a soft smile as she felt part of her heart break for him.

He swallowed hard and took a deep breath whilst squishing his hands beneath his thighs. His watery eyes raised to the top of the tree, giving the decorations the once over. 'I could do with a warm mince pie right about now. Do you fancy one? I could pop a couple in the microwave for a few seconds. I noticed Ashley bought some.' He glanced over at the door as he creaked to a stand. 'She should be back from work soon.'

He had come away from Lapland, so Grace thought it best to join him. 'I'd like one, but I'd really like to get into my PJs now and snuggle on the sofa for the rest of the evening.'

'You okay, Grace?'

'I don't seem to have much energy. I don't feel tired, but my body is acting exhausted. It's quite weird. It's like being tired without being tired. I thought the hot chocolate would perk me up, but it didn't work.'

Charlie squatted to her side. 'You have fatigue. That's what that is. It's not the same as being tired, which is why the sugar-hit failed. How about I help you upstairs and get you ready for the night. You know, Ashley has made a cottage pie for us. It's in the fridge with a bright pink Post-it note stuck to the dish. She is making me laugh with her sticky notes everywhere. I'll put it on later, and we can have our dinner in the living room while watching TV.'

'Sounds like a good plan. I like mine with baked—'

'Beans. Yeah, I know, honey.'

Of course you do. I keep forgetting. You probably know everything about me.

She wondered if she'd told him about the time she fell off the stage at the school Christmas concert when she was fifteen. Her skirt went right over her head, and everyone laughed. That was the most embarrassing moment of her life, that she knew of. She hoped she hadn't done anything embarrassing in the last four years.

I bet I was a right goof when I met you, Charlie Wallis. I can just see myself going giddy for you.

She glanced at the doorway. 'Erm, do you remember how you told me not to lie about my health?' He nodded, looking concerned. 'Well, I'm not sure if I have enough energy to do the stairs.'

Charlie swooped her up into his arms and carried her all the way to their bedroom, where he gently placed her on the edge of the bed before getting on with finding her pyjamas.

Grace went to speak but words clogged at the back of her throat, so she cleared the way and tried again. 'Thank you.'

'Do you want me to help you change? Oh, no, maybe not.' He made the decision before she had a chance to respond. Not that she was going to agree to that level of intimacy. He might be used to it, but she wasn't. 'I'll just go and sort the mince pies, then come straight back to take you downstairs.'

Grace laughed to herself at Charlie fumbling over his own feet in a rush to get out the room.

His voice was muffled on the other side of the bedroom door, but she heard what he said before he went off to the kitchen. 'You started a diary when we got together. It's in the drawer by your side of the bed.'

She quickly looked at the white bedside cabinet and opened the top drawer to see a red notebook and black pen sitting there.

Oh, now he mentions this. Ooh, I'm scared to look. Stop being daft. Pull yourself together, Grace Hadley. Wallis. Oh, just look.

She opened the flap to see it was the diary for the current year. 'Right, let's pick a random page and see where it takes me.' Closing her eyes, she flicked the pages and opened them halfway through the journal. 'Okay, it's May, and…'

Charlie has been working so hard on the late shift. He is worn out, bless him. I lit a whole heap of candles tonight and put them all over the bathroom, then climbed in the bath with him. We made love until the water was cold and we were prunes, but it was wonderful. He's wonderful. I love the way he whispers around my earlobe, telling me he loves me over and over again. Goodness, he melts every part of me when he does that. I think he knows it's one of my favourite things. Well, that and when he…

'Whoa! Grace, what are you writing here? Too much information.' She moved the diary closer and homed in on what it said next.

8

Charlie

Charlie was serving pancakes to Fiona, Harriet, and Lexi in his kitchen, as they had all decided to come unannounced for breakfast. Grace was still in bed, so he wasn't sure yet if her energy had returned. Ashley had already gone off to work, so he thought it would be a nice peaceful morning spent with his wife. The noise in the room created by just three Hadleys was louder than the emergency room at work, but he had got used to Grace's family a long time ago. His own family were pretty quiet in comparison, even though there were five of them altogether. He wasn't sure if all large families were as noisy as his in-laws or if it was just them. Whenever they were together, they seemed to shout more than talk, and he was lucky if he got a word in.

Fiona flapped her hands at her daughters, shushing them for a moment. 'Charlie, how did things go yesterday? Ben called me to say Grace had been up at his farm. Was she okay? Did she remember anything? Were her ribs still hurting?' She turned to Harriet. 'They can take forever to heal, you know. Uncle Mo had terrible arthritis after his fall. I blame that on his ribs.' She gave Charlie a look that pretty much said, *why haven't you spoken yet?*

Charlie handed Lexi the maple syrup and tomato ketchup, because the baby wanted both, apparently.

Harriet screwed up her face as Lexi splodged the sauce over her pancakes. 'That is beyond gross, Lex.'

'I can't help it. Do you know how many bottles of tomato ketchup this baby has gone through? It's ridiculous.' She took in a large mouthful and smiled to herself.

'Never mind her,' said Fiona. 'What about my baby?'

Lexi coughed on her mouthful. 'I am your baby too, you know.'

'I know, dear, but right now you're not important.'

Lexi scoffed and Harriet laughed. 'Cheers, Mum.'

Fiona patted her on the back. 'You know I love you, but shush. Now, Charlie, any news on our Gracie?'

'You could just ask me, Mum.' Grace gave a slight wave at everyone in the kitchen as she slouched in her pink-check PJs in the doorway.

Well, she looks a lot better than she did yesterday, and she's got that sexy bed hair going on. I have to do something about that before I lose the ability to cope.

Charlie kept his laughter inside as he made his way towards her to softly stroke down her blonde hair. Her surprised eyes met his, and, just for a moment, it looked as if they smiled deeply at him.

Do not kiss her. Do not kiss her. Oh wow, this is hard.

'You want some pancakes, Mrs Wallis?' He knew what he was doing as his hand slid slowly down from her hair to her shoulder. He took a step back when a twitch of a smile hit the corner of her mouth.

That's my girl.

He gestured at the kitchen table covered with freshly cooked pancakes, an assortment of condiments, breakfast cereals, and pastries that Fiona had brought. Harriet was pouring out orange juice whilst Lexi was stuffing her face with red pancakes, and Fiona was up out of her chair, taking Grace by the arm to a seat.

'How are you feeling, my baby girl?' asked Fiona, shoving Grace down and filling her a plate with basically everything.

Charlie made her a cup of tea, as he knew she preferred her morning brew before eating anything. She said her thanks and took a sip as he sat by her side to eat his own breakfast, seeing how the Hadleys had been fed.

'I'm okay, Mum. I haven't remembered anything yet, but some things with Charlie have felt sort of familiar. I don't know.' She shrugged and grabbed a shortbread biscuit from a saucer to dunk in her tea.

Charlie swallowed his mouthful of pancake and looked up. 'We have another appointment with Dr Singh next week. Until then, Grace can just rest and hang out with me and see if anything else feels familiar.'

Fiona gave her daughter a sympathetic smile and a light squeeze of the shoulder. 'Is that what you want to do, love?'

Grace nodded and glanced at Charlie. 'I do, Mum. I feel okay here. Plus, Ashley's here all night.' She looked over her shoulder. 'Has she gone to work?'

'Yes,' mumbled Lexi through a mouthful of food. 'But she's left some bits for you to do.'

Charlie gestured towards the boxes piled up along the back wall. 'She thought you might like to help with the toy parcels while you're home today.'

Her eyes widened and almost looked sad. 'Are we home today then?'

'Yeah. Rest day, I'm afraid.' He couldn't help himself. He gently placed a piece of her hair behind her ear. She didn't flinch or move away, so he controlled the nervous breath dying to escape him and went back to eating his breakfast.

Grace looked over at the boxes. 'So, what's this all about then?'

Fiona brought one of the Santa-themed boxes to her, and Grace looked over the shoebox. 'You fill them with the toys and gifts, and we give them out to the children's homes and some of the kids who come to see Santa up at Castle on the Mead. You should see what our Ash has done with the place. Those overgrown gardens are now lovely and trimmed and pruned and whatnot, and Ashley and Harrison have transformed the whole place into a Christmas winter garden for the season. Helps bring in some money, you see.'

Grace shook her head as she handed back the box. 'Sorry, I'm lost. What's Ashley doing working at Castle on the Mead? That place hasn't been open to the public for years. Since when did it have a winter garden going on?'

Harriet laughed. 'Since Ashley starting dating Harrison Connell.'

It sounded like the tea Grace was sipping almost shot up the back of her nose. 'Harrison Connell? Who's Harrison Connell?'

Fiona attempted to mop the spilled tea from Grace's mouth using a piece of kitchen roll. 'The jeweller fella from Gem Walk.' Grace flinched away. 'They got close when Ashley rented one of the shops down there, but the bloke who owns it all sold the lot. You know, that nasty scumbag who got someone to run you down. Viktor Blake. I'm glad he's behind bars. Anyway, Gem Walk will become fancy flats now. Shame. It was always such a lovely ornate type of walkway. I wonder if some of the features are listed.'

'Wait, go back to Ashley,' said Grace, moving her mum's fussing hand further from her face. She looked towards Charlie, who just nodded the confirmation she was obviously after. 'So, that's where she's living now? In a castle with this

65

Harrison Connell, who she failed to mention?' She shook her head as she pushed the remnants of her warm tea out of the way of her plate of food.

'He used to keep himself to himself, until he met us lot.' Fiona wrinkled her nose towards Charlie. 'He's the quiet type. Very well-mannered.'

Grace huffed and waggled a croissant in the air. 'I can't believe you lot. Charlie, why haven't you caught me up on what my sisters are doing nowadays?'

'Why would I know what they get up to?'

'I don't expect intimate details, just the big stuff. You know, like, Ashley lives in a castle.'

Lexi raised a hand before Charlie could speak. 'I live in one of the newbuilds down at Sandly Harbour, with Bryce Silver. I also own Silver Blooms, which Bryce bought for me.'

Charlie felt the need to add the information he did have. 'It's not the old flower shop in Sandly that you know from years ago.'

Grace appeared to throw him a half smile for his attempt. 'I gathered that much, seeing how Bryce turned the building into an office after his aunt died.' She turned back to Lexi. 'Anyway, Heath already filled me in about you, Lex. So, where's the new shop?'

'Pepper Lane.'

'Oh, wow, what a lovely spot. I've always loved Pepper Lane. It would be nice to live down there... Erm...'

Silence loomed for a moment, as no one seemed to know what to say. Fiona spoke first, bringing life back into the kitchen whilst Charlie lowered into his chair.

She still can't get to grips with the fact that Waterside Cottage is her home. This isn't good. I need to up my game. Do more. Make her feel at home. She needs to at least feel at home. But what can I do? I can't turn back time, nor can I fast-forward the future.

He sat silently at the kitchen table, listening to the women chatter on about their lives and everything Grace had forgotten about. Her eyes widened every so often, and there were moments she turned to him for his reaction, so he guessed she must believe he would tell her if anyone was lying. An hour seemed to drag, and he was about to leave them alone when Fiona announced they were leaving, then proceeded to tell Grace she could get started on the Christmas gift boxes.

Charlie saw them to the door, glad of the peace. He was pleased they had visited, but he was always secretly pleased when they left his home, but only because Grace's family were so loud. He went back into the kitchen to find his wife clearing the table.

'Whoa, whoa! Hey, Grace, leave that. I'll do it. You rest.'

She let out a big sigh and flopped down to a chair. 'I'm fed up with rest, Charlie.'

'It's good for you. It's healing.'

'Is that your doctor's opinion?'

He smiled warmly and sat by her side, taking her hand in his. Her skin felt cool and her fingers frail. She stayed with him, gazing down at their connection.

'I'm sorry about earlier, Charlie.'

'What do you mean?'

'When I didn't remember about this place being my home.'

He swallowed the hard lump that appeared in his throat. 'That's okay. Don't stress. It's new to you. Takes some getting used to, that's all.' He scraped his chair closer to her so one of her legs was in between his. 'It's going to be all right, Grace.'

'Will it? What if I never remember?'

'Then we'll make new memories.' He reached up and stroked her hair, and she closed her eyes for a moment, leaning into his hand, causing every part of him to melt. 'You mean everything to me, Grace. You give me life.' He watched her eyes open, and he stared straight into the watery blue glistening his way. 'I want to try something. Are you with me on this experiment?'

Grace bit in her bottom lip and gave a small nod.

Charlie took a breath. 'Okay. Bear with me.' In one swoop, he pulled off his jumper, allowing it to fall to the floor behind him. The fact her eyes widened slightly at his naked chest didn't go unnoticed. He took another breath, this one more controlled, then placed her hand over his heart, with his over hers. He kept eye contact at all times, studying her reaction. Looking for signs of distress, embarrassment, or worse, fear. But her expression was unreadable as she glanced down at their hands amongst his dark chest hair.

'What is this experiment, Charlie?' she asked softly, her voice barely a whisper.

He lowered his head to stare only at their entwined fingers. 'You used to say this was your favourite part of me to touch. You loved to feel my heartbeat, and I would tell you that every time it beats, it beats only for you.' He left his head low but looked up through his lashes. 'It still beats only for you.'

Oh, get a grip, Wallis. Don't cry. Don't you dare cry. Breathe. Just breathe. Easy now.

An almost strangled waft of air escaped his parted lips as Grace placed her forehead down lightly upon his. A teardrop landed on his arm, and he was pretty sure it came from him.

'I don't remember,' she whispered.

'It's okay.' He swallowed, as his words had come out cracked and wounded. It was how he felt, but he wanted to hide his pain from her, for fear of adding more stress to her life.

'But something feels right about touching you.'

Their watery eyes met, and Grace leaned closer and gently kissed his mouth, and there wasn't a place in the world where Charlie's emotions could hide. He breathed out a choked sigh upon her warm lips, wanting so badly to lift her onto his lap and just hold her there, locked with his mouth. But his arms felt weak, his head whirled, and his heart had melted to nothing but mush.

Grace pulled back, looking apologetic. 'I'm not sure if I should've done that.' Her tone was as light as he felt.

'One of the hardest things about this situation is not being able to kiss you whenever I want, and just for the record, I want to kiss you all the time. So, whenever you feel you want to kiss me, or touch me, or just simply hold my hand, you go for it. I would never reject you.'

'I don't know what's right or wrong anymore. My head feels such a mess.'

He leaned forward and gently nudged her nose with his own. 'Follow your heart. It'll take you home.'

'You're so lovely, and I really want this to be real, but I'm struggling. I can see why I fell in love with you, but I don't understand why I'm not in love with you right now.'

He ignored the slap his heart just took and chose to focus on the fact she was being honest with him, and part of that honesty had brought her lips onto his, even if the moment had passed. 'Don't put pressure on yourself to be or feel any way. Just allow whatever comes to come.'

'I'm scared, Charlie.'

So am I. Just the thought of you never loving me again... Argh! I can't think that way. I have to believe. I have to.

'It's okay, honey. I'll always be right here whenever you need me.' He watched as she removed herself from his space, taking herself upstairs to get ready for whatever the day would bring. Charlie just prayed it would bring something she recognised.

9

Grace

Grace read in her diary she was a member of a photography group that met every Tuesday at the local Boy Scouts hut to go walkabout, she assumed to take pictures. She flipped open the laptop she found on a white chest of drawers in her bedroom and sat with it on the bed. There wasn't a password, so she opened the file on the screen that said *Tuesday Pics*. Her eyes widened at the nature shots; she couldn't believe she'd taken such beautiful photographs. The last she knew, she was considering taking a course in the subject, but that was as far as she'd got.

What's this Grace's Certificates malarkey? Ooh, I have qualifications. Looks like I upped my photography game. Well done, me. Shame I can't remember what I learned.

She checked to see if she had any notes from the course. 'Bingo! Looks like one of the courses was online. Yay! I still have all the worksheets. Ooh, I can re-study. What a bummer, but still, onwards and upwards. Plus, it might spark something. Never know.'

Wondering where her camera was, she jumped off the bed to have a shuffle through the bottom of the wardrobe, then peered under the bed and found a black case. She pulled it out, opened it, and was pleasantly surprised to find some rather nice photography equipment.

'Oh, wow. This is mine?' She held up a large telephoto lens, looking it over. 'What on earth do I do with this? Surely I haven't turned into paparazzi.' She carefully placed it on the bed and pulled out the rest. 'Looks like a few quid sitting here. I must have saved hard to buy this lot.'

How am I going to re-join the Tuesday Club if I don't know what I'm doing? Sure, I can take a picture, but...

She picked up the hefty black camera, judging its weight in her hand. The laptop was still open, showing her first module, so she started to speed-read the first page.

Hmm, okay, well, this will help, but do I really want to do this?

She'd always liked photography and often thought about taking it more seriously, but as she studied the camera, she didn't feel excited about making it a career.

Charlie mentioned a studio.

'Let's check that out.'

Every now and then, she had been exploring different parts of the cottage but hadn't ventured to the side extension yet.

Grace lowered the handle on the white wooden door and stepped inside a cool room that had a pasting table set up and little else. She frowned at the magnolia walls, sniffing the air for signs of fresh paint. The only smell she discovered was a dusty one she assumed was coming from the well-used decorating table.

Grace walked over to the French doors to peer outside at the neat garden at the back. There was an old green shed that had some Christmas lights strung up above the door and a stone bird bath close by. She slumped her shoulders as she turned back to the empty room.

'This would make a nice studio.' Her voice seemed to echo in the space.

'You said that the first time you came in here,' said Charlie, standing in the doorway, topless.

Oh, he has that come-to-bed look in his eyes again. It's definitely flattering. He's grinning at me now. That's because I'm staring at his chest.

Grace averted her eyes, looking back at the French doors so she didn't laugh. 'Nice bit of natural lighting in here.'

'Uh-huh.'

She wasn't looking, but she could feel his presence closer to her, and the next thing she knew, he was peering over her shoulder.

'So, Charlie, erm…' She cleared her throat and tried again. 'Did I say anything else when I first came in here?'

Yes, that's way more helpful than staring at his reflection in the glass. Hmm, that would make a good picture.

Charlie's warm breath was close to her neck, causing her to try to control a shiver. 'It wasn't what you said in here that was memorable. It was more what you did.'

She turned to face him, not realising her mouth would be so close to his. The corners of his eyes were creased, and she wasn't sure if he was pausing for dramatic effect or if he wasn't sure whether to say.

'Tell me, Charlie. I'm curious now.'

His eyes left her lips for a second. 'You kind of wanted to christen the room, so to speak.' He laughed quietly as he turned away.

Oh blooming heck. I did it in here with him. Maybe against the French doors. Ooh, steamy windows. Did I pin him to the floor or did he pin me?

She glanced to the middle of the room at the paint-splattered floor, then over at the back wall. Swallowing hard, she attempted to gain control of the stirring in her solar plexus before certain feelings got the better of her, forcing her to turn and latch on to that naked chest of his, with her mouth.

Don't even think about it. Concentrate.

Charlie disturbed the silence and her muddled thoughts. 'I came looking for you because I thought we'd make a start on those Christmas boxes. Then, after lunch, I'm taking you to Edith's Tearoom to make a gingerbread house. I asked Joey if she would bake some gingerbread for us in advance. I know you want to go out, so, it's something sitting down and indoors.'

Thank goodness for the change of subject. I swear sometimes that man can read my mind.

'Erm, you do remember the lady who runs the tea shop in Pepper Lane, Joey Reynolds?'

Grace turned to frown at him. She was getting pretty annoyed with everyone forgetting she had only forgot the last four years. 'Of course I remember... Wait, who? You mean Joey Walker.'

'Oh, yes. She married. She's Reynolds now.'

Grace gasped, slapping one hand over her gaping mouth. 'No way! Did she marry Josh?' She smiled widely, lowering her hand when Charlie nodded. 'Oh, I'm so pleased they got together. She loved him since they were kids. Aww, that's so nice.'

'They had a baby girl this year. Called her Edith. Guess you might get to see her later, if she's about.'

Grace clasped her hands in front of her heart. 'Oh, I'd love that. Thanks, Charlie. And there was me thinking we weren't going out today.'

'Yeah, but I knew you were getting restless. As I said, you'll be sitting down, so it's all good.'

Grace grinned to herself as she left the room, feeling a tad mischievous. 'So,' she called back to him, 'sex in the studio, eh? Hope I did some photograph-worthy moves.' She smiled even wider when she heard him roar with laughter.

'You're teasing me now, honey.'

She laughed to herself as she crossed the hallway. 'Oh, I'm teasing you?' she mumbled, then raised her voice to call out to him. 'Put some bloody clothes on, Charlie Wallis.' His laughter was echoing all around her, and it felt oddly comforting.

10

Charlie

The aroma of ginger was the first thing Charlie and Grace noticed as they entered Edith's Tearoom. Grace sat at a table next to the window and placed her hands on the pink gingham tablecloth whilst Charlie went to the glass counter to order cinnamon hot chocolate for them both.

A pretty blonde lady poked her head out from the back room where the kitchen was. 'Hey, Charlie. I'm just getting your bits together. Go and sit down. I'll bring them over with your drinks. I'll only take a second.'

'That's okay, Joey. Take two.'

Grace was beaming his way as he sat down opposite her. 'Mmm, it smells so good in here. Makes you want to eat the shop.'

Charlie was about to agree when the door opened and someone he didn't like walked in. The tall man in the dark coat hadn't noticed them yet, and Charlie was hoping it would stay that way, but he knew Ewan would spot them soon.

Of all the people to walk in, it had to be him. Charlie had no idea what Grace was going to make of it. She was so heartbroken over Ewan back in the day, she ended up going into a pointless relationship with her friend Freddy.

So, wait, let me work this out. She thought she was still with Freddy when she woke up, and they only stayed together for September and October that year. She broke up with Ewan that June. Great! He really hurt her, and now she's gonna feel that pain as though it's new. I don't know how to... And now he's seen us and is heading this way.

Ewan wrinkled his long nose as he broke into a wide smile. 'Grace. Oh my God. I'm so pleased to see you're okay.'

Charlie watched Grace stand in a daze. She looked unsure and nervous, and he hated seeing her like that. What he hated even more was Ewan pulling her in for a huge hug that lasted way more than a friendly hug should.

'Ewan?' Her voice sounded frail and quite lost, and Charlie clenched his fists tightly on his lap.

Ewan, of course, was four years ahead of Grace. He stepped back, holding her at arm's length, still flashing his pearly whites her way.

'Grace, I didn't think I would see you again till you came back to the club. I'm so glad I came in here today. I did keep asking after you when you were in hospital. I made sure I was caught up on your progress at all times. You look great, by the way.' He leaned forward and kissed her cheek, and Charlie saw the heat rise in her face.

She was clearly struggling with her feelings, and Charlie was struggling with his temper. He knew their backstory, as Grace had told him about all the times Ewan let her down, and how she still went back to him. It was meeting Charlie in December that helped finally burn the bridge between her and Ewan.

Jeez, what's he doing?

Ewan was placing a strand of hair gently behind Grace's ear and taking the opportunity to make sure his knuckle accidently brushed against her cheek.

I'm right here, buddy. I'm gonna smack him one in a minute.

'Ewan, I...' Grace frowned with confusion as she pulled her face away from his wandering fingers that Charlie so desperately wanted to break. 'What club?'

It was Ewan's turn to frown. Obviously he wasn't up-to-date with Grace's condition after all.

Another big fat lie he just told her. Add that to your list, Grace.

'Photography.' Ewan sat at their table as Grace pretty much flopped to her seat. 'Tuesday Club.'

Charlie gave him a death glare, but it went unnoticed, as Ewan was far too busy with his Mr Smooth routine to bother with the likes of Grace's husband.

Seriously, the guy's just gonna pretend I don't exist?

Charlie crossed his arms tightly, then uncrossed them, as he didn't want Grace to see his annoyance. He held his hands back on his lap, safely hidden by the table so nobody could see how tight his grip was.

Ewan leaned forward and angled himself so half his back was facing Charlie, which caused Charlie to raise his eyebrows at the audacity. 'Grace, we go every Tuesday.'

Grace shifted in her chair, clearly uncomfortable. 'Oh, I didn't know you go too. Sorry. Erm... Ewan, I gather no one has filled you in, but I've lost some of my memory. It will probably come back at some point, but for now, I've lost the last four years, so I don't remember going to photography club. I had to read it in my diary to find out. Plus, I've only just discovered I took courses on the subject.' She shrugged coyly. 'Guess I'm going to have to start from scratch.'

Charlie was trying to gauge Ewan's reaction to the news, but it wasn't easy when he could only see half his face. He knew exactly what her ex was thinking though.

Ewan cleared his throat before speaking, and there was a definite smile to his tone. 'Four years, bloody hell, Grace. So, wait, does that mean you think we're still together?'

Charlie's eyes rolled before he had a chance to stop them. Luckily, he managed to swallow down the scoff that attempted to leave his mouth.

'No,' she replied softly. 'I thought I was still with Freddy.' Charlie could see her smile. It was slight and awkward.

'Freddy Morland? You dated him after me? I never knew that.'

'It was just a couple of months.'

'So, our break-up, it's still new to you.' He wasn't asking. He knew, and Charlie could sense his joy.

Grace did the same uncomfortable shrug she had earlier. 'I guess. But I know it was four years ago. I know I'm married now.' Unsure eyes met Charlie, and he smiled warmly, trying for reassurance.

Ewan glanced over his shoulder at Charlie, as though seeing him for the first time. 'Alright, mate.'

Seriously?

Charlie's smile hit level grimace, and Ewan went back to ignoring him.

'Look, Grace, if our break-up is feeling new to you right now, I just want to take this opportunity to say how sorry I am once again.' Ewan nodded slightly. 'I have said that a few times over the years, but you won't remember that.'

How convenient for you, Ewan.

Grace flapped one hand whilst breathing out a huff of a laugh, which Charlie knew was forced. 'Oh, it's okay. Water under the bridge. Obviously, if we go to a club together.'

'You don't go together,' said Charlie at the same time Ewan nodded her way. 'You're just there at the same time.'

Ewan still didn't turn to acknowledge him. 'I was the one who got you interested in photography. You remember that, don't you, Grace?' She pulled her lips in and nodded. 'We're good friends nowadays. We always have a great time at the club. You will come back now you're better, won't you?'

'She's not better yet,' said Charlie. And suddenly all eyes were on him. Unlike Grace, he wasn't about to fall apart at the seams every time blue-eyed wonder-boy made puppy-dog eyes whilst staring at his lips.

The two men locked eyes, and Charlie could see Ewan's hatred towards him, stemmed by pure jealousy.

Really, dude?

Ewan's wide mouth twisted to one side. 'I think she's old enough to make up her own mind about what it is she's ready for, Doc.'

'I, erm...' Whatever Grace was thinking, the words died in her mouth. Her face had paled, and Charlie knew he needed to focus on her, which meant controlling the need to punch Mr McSmirky in his smirky face.

'She's to take it easy for now. Doctor's orders.'

Ewan's smirk had set like the Botox in his forehead. 'Is that right?'

Charlie leaned forward, placing his crossed arms on the table. 'Yeah, it is.'

'I'm sure getting out and about will do her some good. You should know that, what with you being a so-called doctor.'

'She is out and about.' Charlie gestured her way. 'See.'

Ewan turned back to Grace. 'I can always pick you up if you want to come. I'll drop you home too, so you wouldn't have to worry about jumping on the bus or anything. That's what got you knocked down in the first place, having to always get the bus. I'd help you, Grace. You can rely on me.'

Charlie wasn't entirely sure if a sarcastic laugh had left his mouth or stayed inside his mind. Either way, neither of them were paying him any attention. Grace had her polite smile on, and Ewan was entering her personal space.

'I'll think about it, Ewan. Thanks for the offer.'

Joey's voice boomed across the tea shop. 'Ewan, black coffee to go, is it?'

He finally took his eyes off Grace. 'Yep, ta.' He stood, bowed slightly, kissed the top of Grace's head, then made his way to the counter to pay for his drink.

Joey smiled over at Charlie. 'I'll be right with you.'

Charlie shuffled closer to the table to talk to Grace, but in two long strides, Ewan had managed to beat him to it.

'Here's my card, Grace. In case you can't find my number.' He handed it over and gave her shoulder a quick squeeze.

I swear to God, if he touches her one more time...

'Call me any time,' Ewan added. 'I'll always be here for you, babe.'

Grace was studying his card, clearly an attempt to avoid eye contact. Charlie knew all her little ways, and he could see how much seeing Ewan again wasn't easy for her.

Ewan left, and Joey brought over a large tray filled with a flatpack gingerbread house and all the accessories needed to decorate. She placed it on the table next to them, smiled sympathetically at Charlie, then gave Grace a huge hug.

'Good to see you, Grace. Charlie filled me in over the phone. So, four years, eh? And then Ewan. That's all you need.' She placed one hand on Charlie's shoulder, keeping her taupe eyes on Grace. 'Good thing you've got this one in your corner now.'

Grace smiled at Charlie, warming him instantly, then she turned to Joey. 'I heard you married Josh Reynolds and had a baby girl.' Joey nodded. 'That's great news, Jo. I'm so happy for you.'

Joey scanned the table. 'Hey, didn't I make your hot chocolate?' She shook her head at herself. 'I think I still have baby brain, or maybe it's sleep deprivation. My gran told me that once you have kids, you never deep sleep again. It's true. I can't believe how much of a light-sleeper I am now. The slightest noise wakes me. Anyway, let me just get your drinks. Cinnamon, right?'

Charlie nodded as Grace confirmed the order. He grabbed her hand across the table as she went to reach out for the silver cake board. He held it gently within his own whilst keeping eye contact, trying to read her mind.

'Are you okay, Charlie?' A pinkness had returned to her cheeks, and her voice didn't sound as cracked as it did around Ewan.

Charlie leaned over and kissed her knuckles. 'I'm looking forward to building our new home together.' He gestured over at the gingerbread house pieces.

She smiled widely. 'At least we can eat this one.'

'Well, if at any time you feel the need to take a bite out of the doorframe at Waterside Cottage, I won't tell anyone.'

She laughed, and the stale air that Ewan had caused was back to smelling as sweet as the cinnamon Joey was sprinkling into their drinks.

'You, erm, thinking about going back to Tuesday Club, Grace?'

She glanced his way, looking unsure how she should respond.

'It's okay if you want to go. You always enjoyed it so much.'

'Just how friendly am I with Ewan these days?'

'Well, it took you a while to get over him. Hanging out with Freddy helped, but then we met that December, and...'

She took her hand back from his to point at him. 'Doctor Love.'

They shared a laugh, then he placed some more of the gingerbread pieces in front of them.

'Seriously, though, Charlie. Was I still pining after him when I met you?'

'No, Grace. You were too busy falling in love with me.' He placed a hand over his heart and grinned with mock surprise.

'So you healed me, did you?'

'No, honey. You did that all by yourself the day you decided never to go back to him again.' The hint of pride that flittered in her eyes didn't go unnoticed, and he liked that she was feeling pretty pleased with herself.

He just had to hope she wouldn't fall under Ewan's spell once again. Everything about the snake told Charlie that he was ready to try and win Grace back, and Charlie was smart enough to know that with the way things were, Ewan might be in with a chance.

11

Grace

Grace had spent a couple of days tucked up indoors, roasting marshmallows in the open fireplace, listening to Christmas songs, making mince pies with Ashley in the evenings, and Christmas cookies during the day with Charlie. She had played Cluedo, Connect Four, and Go Fish, watched a few Hallmark movies, and spent time catching up with her diary, which got a touch steamy in places, causing her to gape at some of her own descriptions, plus, visualisations of Charlie's bare chest to appear.

She gazed out a bedroom window at the small pond in the front garden, wondering if the wildlife was snuggled away like her. She was starting to get a bit stir crazy.

The Donkey Sanctuary needed all hands on deck during the festive season, as everyone wanted to see a donkey at Christmas, and Grace's favourite donkey, Mistletoe, was probably wondering where she had gone. As far as she was concerned, the donkeys needed her to get back to work.

Grace hadn't had any fatigue the last couple of days. She figured she'd be okay. The Donkey Sanctuary was calling, and Charlie would just have to deal with it.

She pulled her blue-check shawl further around her shoulders, wrapping herself tightly, and made her way to the kitchen to find Charlie clearing up the breakfast mess.

'Charlie, I'm going out.'

He glanced over his shoulder from the sink. 'Where are you going, honey?'

For some reason, Grace felt annoyed that he hadn't put up a fight. His voice was soft and carefree as though everything was perfectly normal. She really thought she would have to be firm and put him in his place. She was fed up being told what to do or where she could go. It was time to make a stand.

'I'm going over to the Donkey Sanctuary to see if they need me to start back. I know I get whacked out quickly, but I could still lend a hand. They get really busy this time of year. Maybe I could put in some hours, even if it's just two a day.' She was studying his eyes as she spoke, but they were still soft and gentle. No fight there. 'Or I could go in a couple of days a week.' She shrugged, not knowing what else to add. Charlie's relaxed demeanour was slightly off-putting.

'Sure, okay. No harm in seeing what your boss says. Would it be okay if I came too?'

Ah, there it is. I knew he had something up his sleeve. That's why he was calm about me going out.

'I don't need babysitting, Charlie.'

He tilted his head to one side in mock hurt. 'Hey, Grace, I don't want to come as your babysitter. I want to go places with you because I'm your husband and I like spending time with you.'

A corner of her heart melted against her wishes. He was always so lovely to her, and she wasn't always sure she deserved such affection when she wasn't returning the gesture.

She twiddled with the edge of her shawl as her left foot started to fidget. 'I, erm… Sure. If you want. You don't have to hang out with me all the time though. I don't expect that.'

'I always hang out with you when I'm not working. You're my home, Grace. Where else would I want to be?'

Oh crumbs, he's beyond adorable.

She remembered reading in her diary about how she thought he should be in a Hallmark film, as he definitely was the dream-come-true type.

She swallowed hard, realising she was staring at his chest. At least this time he had a top on. 'Okay then.'

He tossed a tea towel over to the worktop and kissed her head as he passed her by. 'I'll just get our wellies out. We usually put them in the boot and change when we get there.'

Grace followed him to the hallway, where two sets of dark-green wellies made an appearance from a nearby coat closet. A distinct smell of dusty straw filled her nostrils and a feeling of déjà vu struck whilst she watched Charlie sitting on the bottom step of the staircase, pulling on his black walking boots.

He stood, offering her red coat, obviously noticing the way she was staring into space. 'You okay?'

'Hmm? Oh, yeah. Fine.' Grace wrapped up for the chill outside and took over the task of loading the boot with whatever Charlie said they needed.

She leaned against the yellow beetle, watching him lock the front door. Her brow was tight and her eyes narrow.

What is it that I'm feeling?

She got in the car as soon as he turned to head her way. There was no way she wanted him knowing she was staring at him again. She had lost count of the number of times she found herself doing that. It was bad enough she didn't remember him, she didn't feel the need to add *weirdo* to the list.

The car ride over to the Donkey Sanctuary was slow and steady, and Charlie hardly said a word. She gathered he was giving her some space in his own way, as she wasn't exactly filled with conversation.

A smile crept on Grace's face as they pulled up in the car park of one of her favourite places. Ever since she left school, she had worked with the donkeys. Even if she was a millionaire, she would still volunteer her time at the Donkey Sanctuary. The animals were her friends, and the staff an extension of her family. The only time she was sad at work was when a donkey died or a rescue came in that really needed all the love she had inside her.

She climbed out the car and inhaled her surroundings. The cool air wafted over her pale face, reddening her cheeks and clearing out her sinuses. Charlie handed her a tissue from his pocket and she blew her nose whilst still smiling.

'I love this place, Charlie.'

'I know you do, honey.'

She stuffed the tissue into her pocket and pointed over at the entrance. 'Look at all the tinsel and bows.' She laughed out a waft of cold air. 'I'm sure that's way more than we usually put up.'

'It's looks very sparkly.' He nudged her arm. 'Come on.'

Grace got as far as opening the main door when a young man flew into her arms.

'Oh, G-Girl. I'm so happy you're here. I've missed you, my sister from another mister.' He flailed his hands over his head and whooshed around in a circle in a botched pirouette that almost toppled him over. He straightened, flicked back his long blond hair, and grinned with all the cheekiness of a five-year-old.

'Oh, Sidney, it's so good to see you too. I'm so ready to come back to work.'

Sidney wrinkled his button nose and stretched his dark eyes. 'Darling, I don't think Red will let you back on the roster just yet. You've not long come out of hospital. Put your feet up, I say. Enjoy the time off.'

Grace peered around him at the small, dark-wood reception desk. 'Where is she? I'll tell her.'

'Oh please, don't tell her. You know what she's like. You have to ask her. Beg. Plead. Grovel, if you must.' He clapped his hands in excitement. 'Ooh, what a fab Crimbo it's going to be this year with you back in the game, or in our case, stable.'

'Is that Hadley?' called a rough, throaty voice from the back room behind the desk. A head poked out, revealing bunched-up, wiry ginger hair and a flushed face. The fifty-seven-year-old woman came out to hug Grace and slap her back. 'You scared the bloody living daylights out of me, young lady. Don't ever do that again.'

Grace huffed out a laugh. 'Well, I'll certainly try not to, Red.'

Red whacked Grace's right shoulder, causing her to jolt forward a step. 'Now, what's all this I hear about memory loss? We can't have that. Do you know your way around a donkey, Hadley?'

Grace lifted one hand to cover her mouth in mock amusement. 'Gosh, well, I think I might just know where to pin the tail.'

'Oh, haha, very funny. So, what you doing here today?' Red turned her beady green eyes to Charlie, looking as though she were about to kick him out. 'Why are you both here?'

Sidney answered before anyone else had a chance to draw breath. 'Grace wants to come back to work. Isn't that fab?'

Red shot him a stern glare that caused Sidney to poke his tongue out at her when she turned back to eyeball Grace. 'No, it is not fab. You're not working yet, Hadley. Take the month off. Eat mince pies or something, just go home. I have enough on my plate without having to worry about you feeding the donkeys pickled onions because you don't know what you're doing.'

Grace rolled her eyes. 'I haven't forgotten how to handle donkeys, Red. I'm bored, okay. I want to work.' She quickly turned to Charlie. 'Oh, no offence.'

He showed his gloved palms. 'None taken.'

Great, now he thinks I don't like his company, or he's boring or something.

Red huffed and went back to the desk. 'It's settled, Hadley. You don't start back till the new year. Take it or leave it.'

'But—'

'Nope.'

Grace dropped her shoulders in defeat. If there was one thing she could remember, it was just how stubborn Red was. She turned to see Sidney's face had fallen flatter than her own. She rubbed his arm to help comfort him, knowing he hated working without her around.

Red bellowed over at Sidney, making him jump. 'Sid, aren't you supposed to be somewhere with Star?'

He crossed his arms in a huff and frowned at her. 'That's not till after lunch.'

'It's late morning. Go get her ready now.'

Sidney gave a mock salute and swirled on his tiptoes to head off to a doorway to his right. 'I'm going, I'm going. Laters, G-Girl. You too, Hot Doc.'

Charlie wrinkled his brow. 'Does everyone call me that?'

Grace went over to Red. 'Where's Star going?'

'Hadley, you don't work here at the moment, so just go visit the donkeys, then go home.' Red went into the back room and closed the door.

Charlie pointed over at the desk. 'Is she always like that?'

'Yep. But you get used to her. She loves us all, really.' She smiled widely and gestured towards the doorway Sidney had used. 'Come on. I really do need to see Mistletoe. She'll be missing me.' She glanced back at Charlie following her through the tinsel-adorned doorway. 'I'm her favourite, you see. I used to stay up all night with her when she first arrived. She was so scared, bless her.'

'Yeah, I remember you telling me all about your favourite donkey on our first date.'

Grace stopped walking to turn and laugh. 'That's what I talked about on our first date?'

'Hey, I spoke about a burst appendix and the woman who tried to eat a brick. It's what we do, right? Talk about our life. Get to know someone.'

Grace skipped over everything they had both said and went straight for the bizarre brick story. 'Someone tried to eat a brick?'

He took her hand and walked with her to the stables. 'Yeah. It was an extreme pregnancy craving. It got quite messy. Broken teeth. Blood.'

'Wow, you deal with some crazy stuff down at A&E.'

'You can say that again.'

Full-on donkey aroma filled the air as Grace entered the long line of stables to see Sidney at the end, brushing down Star. She gave a slight wave, then approached Mistletoe, who nuzzled her nose into Grace's outstretched hand.

'Hello, my beaut. Did you miss me? I missed you.' She kissed the donkey, then smiled up at Charlie, who was looking around at the large red bows stuck on the walls away from the animals. 'Come on, Mistletoe, let's go for a walk.' She opened the stable door and gestured to Charlie to follow her outside to a large paddock.

'Erm, Grace, don't you need to put a harness on her or something?'

She shook her head and flashed him a confident smile. 'Nah, not this one. Mistletoe walks when I walk, stops when I stop, and comes when I call her.'

'Wow, she's like a well-trained dog.'

Grace giggled. 'Yeah, but I didn't train her. She just does it, but only with me. Oh, and if she nudges you with her nose, don't feel offended. She does it with anyone who comes too close to me, except children. She doesn't get jealous of them.'

'Oh, well, that's handy to know.' Charlie scrunched his nose as Grace breathed out a laugh, and Mistletoe side-eyed him, causing Charlie to side-step away. 'I can't believe I'm in competition with a donkey for my wife's affection.'

Her first instinct was to tell him he had no competition, but the words failed to leave her, and she wasn't even sure why she'd had that thought. She simply lowered her head until she placed Mistletoe inside the paddock and closed the gate. 'Mistletoe likes to be in the enclosure. It makes her feel safe.'

I feel safe in Waterside Cottage. I wish I could remember what I felt like the day I moved in.

Charlie leaned by her side, and the fresh smell of a light citrus aftershave made her turn his way. 'Come on.' She gestured behind them to a small café next to a wooden hut that housed a giant nativity display overlooking the paddock. 'Let's sit outside and have a cuppa and a slice of ginger loaf.'

Charlie followed her and sat on one of the metal chairs whilst she headed inside to serve herself, as no one was around and she knew where everything was and how to work the old tea and coffee machine that was sure to explode one day.

Grace felt her heart warm as she washed her hands, then set about slicing the cake and making their tea. Without even thinking about it, she added milk but no sugar to Charlie's tea and just half a teaspoon of white sugar to her own. She grabbed a handful of mini speculoos biscuits from a glass jar and tossed them on a saucer, then placed everything on a wooden tray and headed back outside.

'Mmm,' groaned Charlie, tucking into the ginger loaf straight away. 'I remember when you introduced me to this cake. Who makes it? Do you know? I've just realised I've never asked.'

'Nora. Sidney's gran. She has always made them for here. Always goes down well.'

'You often bring some of this home.'

'Have I not brought you here before, Charlie?'

'I've visited on occasion. Picked you up and dropped you off, but mostly I go off to work and leave you to it. I don't tend to hang around with the donkeys, and you don't hang around in A&E.'

Grace sipped her tea whilst staring over at a mooching Mistletoe, who was sniffing around another donkey, Angel. She wanted to talk to Charlie about Tuesday Club, but she wasn't sure how to approach the subject.

Come on, just spit it out. He's your husband, so you can't be afraid to say things. Not to him, else what's the point of being with him.

That was what her life was like with Ewan. Walking on eggshells wasn't something she was prepared to do again. She didn't want to be afraid to speak to Charlie about anything.

'Charlie, I was thinking about going to photography club tomorrow evening. I'd like to see my friends there, even if I can't remember them. Well, you know, except for Ewan.'

She watched his chest rise and fall steadily. 'I don't really want to take the bus, so I was wondering if you wouldn't mind dropping me off. I know Ewan offered, but I'm not sure I want to call him to—'

'I'll take you.' He lowered his fork, giving the impression he had lost his appetite. 'And I'll pick you up too. Is that okay?'

'Yes. I'd appreciate that. I appreciate everything you do for me, Charlie. Just so you know.'

'You're welcome.'

Well, that was easy.

It was obvious in Edith's Tearoom that Charlie wasn't exactly keen to breathe the same air as Ewan, but Grace was sure he didn't feel threatened by her ex. Charlie did something Ewan never did. He made her heart smile. Everything felt oddly okay whenever she looked at her husband. He was up there with Santa. Friendly. Kind. Safe.

She nudged his plate back towards him, offering a warm smile. 'Finish your cake.'

12

Charlie

Charlie drove up to the small castle Ashley's boyfriend, Harrison, owned. The grounds at Castle on the Mead had been transformed into a winter garden for the month of December, bringing Christmas cheer to all its visitors. Tall Victorian streetlamps dressed with red-berry wreaths lined a long winding driveway that led up to the large door of the old building. Two six-foot, red, gold, and blue Nutcrackers stood on guard either side of the twinkling garland-adorned arched doorway, and a huge Christmas tree decorated with multicoloured lights and giant red, gold, and blue baubles was on display in the middle of a round flowerbed on the front lawn.

Harrison greeted Charlie at the door, offering a large red mug filled with orange-flavoured hot chocolate, which Charlie was grateful to hold just to warm his hands.

'Ashley said you were on your way here. She's in one of the back rooms, holding court.'

Charlie breathed a laugh into his drink. 'Holding court?'

'Staff meeting.' He glanced at his watch. 'Although everyone should be taking their places soon. We start getting more visitors after seven during the weekdays. I think people like to have their dinner, then come for a walk around the grounds to see the lights. We're hoping for more customers once the kids break up from school.'

Charlie went to stand next to the stone fireplace, as he was feeling a chill in his bones. He was looking forward to a long soak in the tub when he got home, but he had to wait till nine to pick up Grace from photography club. 'Yeah, I heard you got yourself a Santa here.'

Harrison nodded, gesturing towards a dark-wood door at the far end of the hallway. 'Ashley's idea. We've designed a room to look like a workshop fit for North Pole elves. The kids will love it, hopefully. Come on, I'll show you while there's no one there, and it'll help keep your mind occupied.'

Charlie followed him across the hall whilst huffing out a laugh. 'Who says I need my mind occupied?'

Harrison flashed him a smile. 'Ash told me Grace has gone out alone for the first time since leaving hospital.' He shrugged and opened a door that led to a long corridor. 'I'd feel the same, if it were me, but Grace will be all right. She just wants to get back to normal, that's all. I know how it feels. I'm the same whenever I come out of hospital. I don't want fuss either. Just normality.'

As an A&E doctor, Charlie had seen many burns and scars over the years, but Harrison was the only person he had met who'd been disfigured due to an acid attack. He had heard of it happening to people but to see first-hand the damage it had caused to half of Harrison's face was truly heartbreaking. It was in his nature to help fix people, but there wasn't anything he could do to help Harrison except give him reassuring comments every so often about how well his skin was looking since his latest operation.

Harrison raised one eyebrow as he side-eyed his doctor friend. 'You studying my face again, Charlie?'

Charlie smiled warmly, offering his best bedside manner. 'Oh, you know I'm always fascinated by how well your face is doing.'

'Yeah, it's pretty amazing what they can do nowadays.' Harrison ruffled his light-brown hair and grinned. 'Shame they can't fix my hair.'

Charlie laughed. 'There's nothing wrong with your hair.'

'It's thinning by the day. And if I recede any more, I think I'm going to shave the lot off and own the bald look.'

Charlie sipped his hot drink, inhaling the orange scent. 'Mmm, this is good.'

'Thank you. We're selling hot drinks in our shop.'

'You two really have brought this old place back to life. My aunt used to come up here years ago. She always liked the place. She's into gardens.'

'A lot of people are. We've still got a lot of work to do here, which we'll probably get into more in the new year, but we figured if we set a festive theme about the place, it'll help with the funding for the quieter months. Plus, Ashley wanted something nice and Christmassy ready for when Grace woke from the coma. Hey, look at this.'

Charlie smiled at the large red postbox marked *Santa's Letters and Wishes*. He stroked over the handknitted reindeer hat spread over the top, feeling the softness of the wool.

I know what I wish for this year. Dear Santa, please bring back Grace's memory.

Charlie silently exhaled. 'I miss being a kid sometimes. My life was way more simple back then.'

'Yep, mine too. Anything before twenty-two, for me.'

Charlie knew that was how old Harrison was when a jealous ex-boyfriend of the girl he was dating threw acid in his face. He lightly tapped his shoulder. 'Hey, H, life has some weird ups and downs, right?'

Harrison agreed. 'Every time I look at Ashley, I'm blown away. I really can't believe my luck.'

Charlie's heart warmed with thoughts of Grace. 'Yeah, I know that feeling.'

Harrison grinned, breathing out a small laugh. 'They're a loud bunch, though, those Hadleys, eh?'

Charlie stopped laughing when Harrison opened a door to reveal Santa's workshop. He recognised some of the Christmas shoeboxes sitting on the shelves, the same ones he had in his house.

Harrison picked one up. 'We're doing a send-a-gift charity with some of these. We're asking parents to buy a box, and their kids get to pick out a few bits to put inside, then we send them to the children's homes we're collaborating with.' He put down the box to hold up a pair of pyjamas. 'We've got some clothing too. We know how old the kids are in three of the care places, so we've kind of bought some pieces that match each child. We rang around and got a lot of donations too. So, the young visitors we get here will think they're helping the elves. And, yeah, Ashley's got a couple of local teens to dress up while working here at weekends. We'll go full-time with Santa once the kids break up.'

Charlie carefully placed his finished drink down on a red workbench so he could walk around the colourful workshop to look at all the toys. 'That's a great idea, H. I'm bringing Grace up here in a couple of days for the full treatment. We'll definitely buy a Christmas box.'

'Thanks. Hey, come up on Sunday. We've got carriage rides that day. Lucky Riding Stables will be taking people around the outskirts of the castle. We made a deal with Rhett over there to go halves on all income. She's got the magical carriage, and we've got a castle. What's more romantic than that?'

'Grace is gonna love that. Yep, I'm looking forward to our date here.'

I wonder how she's getting on. No prizes for guessing Ewan will try to be her knight in shining armour all night.

'Tell Ashley to keep quiet. I want to surprise Grace with the carriage ride. We'll come up early evening. That way, we can enjoy the last of the daylight here and then night-time.'

'My lips are sealed.' Harrison pulled his pinched fingers across his mouth and winked. He sat on a blue bench, leaned on the table, and waited till Charlie's eyes came his way.

Charlie's brow tightened. 'What?'

'Just want to know how you're doing, Doc. Even though I'm not your patient, you're always checking on me whenever you see me.'

'I'm okay.'

'That's good to know.' Harrison patted the bench, gesturing for Charlie to sit. 'But now be honest. And this is coming from a grown man who I know you've seen cry. So, if I can reveal my feelings, you can too.'

Charlie inhaled deeply, feeling his lungs tighten from stress. Everything about him felt tight and in need of a two-week holiday, preferably floating in the Dead Sea. He sat opposite Harrison whilst rubbing his hand across his forehead, only to get tangled in his dark hair. He tugged his fingers free and flopped his shoulders. 'It's just a long road, H. That's all. It would be tough on anyone.'

'What are you doing to release the stress?'

'Running, mostly. Working, a lot. Well, I was when Grace was in a coma. Now, I don't know what I'm doing half the time. Winging it.' He shook his head slightly, not knowing what to add, as he wasn't entirely sure how he was feeling. Jealous was a top contender since Ewan had made an appearance.

Charlie needed to stop thinking about Ewan and Grace. She'd been in the same club as her ex for ages, and it never bothered him before, but now he didn't know what level she was at with Ewan. He certainly knew what level Ewan wanted to be at with Grace, and there was no way he was going to let that happen.

'How's it going with Grace?'

'Oh, slow. Hey, sorry about keeping Ashley away from you. I was hoping Grace would feel comfortable enough by now to live with just me. I keep forgetting that, in her mind, I'm pretty much a stranger.'

'Don't worry about me and Ash. We're okay. Grace is priority right now. Plus, when you think about it, Ashley has still been coming here a lot to work, and Grace has been fine with that. It's mostly bedtime Grace seems to need her around.'

'Yeah, because she's afraid to be left in the house overnight with me.'

Harrison started putting some Lego pieces together that were in a box to his side. 'She's not afraid, Charlie. Something deep inside her will tell her there's nothing to be afraid of.'

'You think?'

'Yep. We all have gut instincts. Grace will get a sense of things. I'm sure.' He paused and smiled. 'That includes what Ewan is really like.'

Charlie tilted his head to one side along with his lips. 'And why have you brought up Ewan?'

'If Ashley's concerned about him trying to wheedle his way back into Grace's life, then I know you'll be feeling the same way.'

'Ashley is concerned?'

'She just doesn't like him, that's all. You know what Ash is like. She has little trust towards most people, let alone anyone who dares to date one of her sisters.'

Charlie had to agree. 'She is very protective over the people she loves. She was the only one who scared me when I first met the family.'

Harrison belly laughed, then glanced over his shoulder at the red tinsel-lined window, seeing if she was there. 'Ah, she's as soft as a kitten once you get to know her.'

Charlie's face broke out into a big smile. 'I so know you were scared of her before you started dating.'

Harrison flapped one hand. 'Hey, the whole family scared me. Shh!'

Charlie huffed and lowered his head into his hands as he rested his elbows on the table, jolting only when his elbow wobbled on a piece of Lego. 'Right now, the only thing that scares me is losing my wife.'

'You won't lose her. Just keep doing what you're doing. Something must be working. After all, she hasn't gone back to her mum's yet.'

That's a valid point.

'Grace never did quit anything straight away. She always gives everything her all, and she did promise to give our relationship a shot.'

And then there was that kiss. Oh jeez, I cannot think about that. She's killing me. She's actually killing me.

Harrison tapped his arm, gaining attention. 'Ashley told me Christmas is your thing, so maybe it's a sign she woke up just in time to spend it with you.'

'I never thought of it like that. Christmas is our time. That's why I'm taking her to places that are full-on Christmas themed. Something has to jog her memory. A smell, a scene, a shared hog roast. Something. Anything. I'm really trying, Harrison, but so far, nothing.'

'Nothing at all?'

'Well, sometimes she says something feels familiar, or I see a look in her eyes, as if she's picking up on something, but she's struggling. You know, like when you have something on the tip of your tongue.'

Harrison nodded and smiled. 'I think that sounds good. Does she have a head doctor? Someone she sees about progress?'

'If you mean a neurologist, then yeah. She's also been offered counselling, but she's still thinking that over. Grace has never been one to take help easily. She's the giver not taker. She's always been the one who looks out for everyone else. Eldest child, see.'

'I learned how to look after myself a long time ago, so I know how hard it is to suddenly have others step forward to offer a hand. All you can do is be there for her. She's only human, after all. She'll need more support than she realises. It might just take her a bit more time to see that. Independent people are the worst when it comes to asking for help.'

'She never had any boundaries with me. From the moment we met, we hit it off, and it was as though we knew each other already. She told me her deepest fears and darkest secrets. You don't share that kind of info with people unless you trust them completely. We had that kind of companionship. It was so easy. We just worked. And now, well, now I don't know what we have. I get that it's different for her this time. I know she's confused, but—'

'Hey, Charlie. It's going to work itself out. When you met, you connected straight away, so that kind of bond will fight its way through. You've got to focus on that. Trust in your love, okay?'

Charlie found himself nodding, even though he wasn't completely convinced. 'I really hope so, Harrison, because this hurts like nothing I've ever experienced before.'

13

Grace

Ewan's wide smile was the first thing Grace saw as she entered the old Boy Scouts hut in Sandly. As he was the only face she recognised out of the small group all looking her way, she was pleased to see he didn't hold any awkwardness in his expression. That was just her.

She wasn't sure if she should act as though she knew everyone. She felt like the out-of-town cowboy who had just walked into the saloon.

I'm going to assume I made friends, especially with that old man with the grey beard. He looks interesting, like someone I would gravitate towards.

'Grace, you're back.' A tall thin woman thumped into her chest, hugging her so tightly, Grace could hardly breathe. 'I was super excited when I heard you were up and about.' Her big brown eyes glanced at Ewan. 'And when Ewan said you might return to group, well, we were all eagerly awaiting more news.' She wriggled a long bony finger at the back wall. 'Oh, if we had known it would be today, we would have put up a sign.' She nodded to the two men sitting by a radiator, twiddling with camera parts that Grace had yet to learn about. 'We spoke about a welcome-back party, didn't we, everyone?'

The old man with the grey beard stepped forward to clasp Grace's hand in his. Beady blue eyes smiled warmly as his cold fingertips welcomed her back. 'Grace, you look well, my love. Now, tell me, do you remember any of us?' He gave a slight nod as his smile stretched. 'It's okay. We heard about your memory loss.' Without taking his eyes from hers, he spoke to the room. 'But we're all here to help, right, everyone?'

The two sitting men stood and came over to say hello. The short stocky one gently patted her shoulder blade whilst the young lad with the long blond hair pulled in his thin lips and nodded.

Grace held a blush she couldn't control. 'I'm sorry, but I don't remember any of you, except Ewan, of course.'

The old man blew out a laugh Santa would have been proud of. 'That's okay. We were expecting this.' He removed himself from her view so he could introduce everyone. 'I'm Walter, and this young lady is Veronica.'

Veronica, who looked around the age of fifty, lightly tapped his arm as she giggled. She flicked back the multicoloured foil strands weaved into her dark hair and beamed at Grace. 'He's such a tease. I'm fifty-seven and counting.'

Walter grabbed her arm, locking it with his own, and embraced Veronica into his frail body. 'Everyone is young when you get to my age.' He turned to wink at Grace. 'Eighty-one and no longer counting.'

Oh, everyone here seems so lovely. I can see why I liked coming here. Now, if only I knew how to talk photography, I might blend in a bit more.

Walter gestured towards the two men. 'This here is Derek, and the young lad there with the rock star hair is Junior.' He stared over at the door as the men greeted Grace once again. 'We have another member, Alice, but she doesn't always come.'

Veronica squeezed Walter's arm closer to her as her eyes widened at Grace. 'Depends if her husband lets her play out.'

Walter frowned. 'Now, now, Veronica. Gossip is never a good thing.' He let go of her arm and headed over to a small table that held tea, coffee, and biscuits. 'I'll make you a tea, Grace. Don't worry, I know just how you like it.'

Veronica filled his space, snuggling even further up to Grace. 'Take no notice of him. Gossip is always a good thing. I will fill you in. By the end of class, you'll be up to speed, especially on Timid Alice and her gobby old man.' She lightly nudged her elbow. 'Hey, who knows, all the old gossip might even help you remember something. I'm sure you'll remember me soon enough. I've always been told I'm quite memorable.'

Grace couldn't help but smile at her new/old friends. The atmosphere in the small wooden hut was upbeat, warm, and made her feel right at home.

Junior held up his chunky camera. 'It's too cold to go walkabout tonight, so we're just going to see what we can snap around the perimeter. Did you bring your camera?' He glanced to her side at her small beige handbag hanging off her shoulder.

'Erm, about that.' Grace raised her voice a touch so Walter could hear from across the room. 'I can't remember any of the photography skills I learned over the last four years, so I'm back to basics, I'm afraid.' She opened her bag and pulled out a small pearl-pink camera she used to use for holiday snaps.

Derek gave it the once over, scrunching his pudgy nose whilst sliding the shutter back and forth a few times as though once wasn't enough. 'This will do. For now. But, Grace, you're good. We need to get you back in the game.'

'I'm reading over my old course notes, and I still have access to assignments online. Hopefully, I'll be a fast learner.'

Ewan's arm suddenly appeared around her shoulders, causing the slightest of shivers to run along her spine, and not in any good way. 'You've always been smart, Gracie. You'll pick this back up in no time.' Her eyes flinched as his nose appeared to nuzzle the top of her hair.

Veronica took her hand and pulled her towards the refreshments table. 'Come and sip your tea first. I had to hold mine just to bring back some circulation in my fingers.' She glanced at the small square window above the table. 'Jeez, it's cold out there tonight.' She tugged Grace's cream scarf. 'Good to see you're well wrapped.'

I don't think Charlie would have let me out otherwise. I'm surprised he didn't put cotton wool all over me. Blimey, I'll be like that Alice they mentioned. They'll talk about me next. The woman who had to get a permission slip from her old man. I wonder what Charlie is doing now.

She felt Ewan's body touch her back as he leaned over to pick up a chocolate bourbon from the packet sitting next to an old green kettle that really had seen better days.

'Right, I'm heading outside,' called Derek, slouching towards the door, with his eyes only on his camera.

'Yeah, me too,' said Junior, hot on his heels.

Veronica smiled sweetly at Grace. 'What do you want to do tonight, my lovely? You could stay in the warm if you like.' She huffed to herself as she grimaced at her surroundings. The old hut had little going on inside. Some stacked tables and chairs along one wall, a dark-wood piano, some gym mats, and a small side room that led to one toilet. 'Not that it's overly warm in here. They really could do with better heating.'

Grace followed her eyes around the room, taking in what it had to offer. 'Well, I saw an album of mine filled with plant pictures, so I thought I could start with that. I'll pop outside too. See what I can find around this hut.'

'Good plan. The boys have some lights outside, so feel free to use them.' Veronica headed to the side room. 'I'm just nipping to the loo before I head out. You take your time, Grace. Find your bearings. You'll be back to your old self soon enough, I know. I can feel it in my water. Speaking of which.' Her pace sped up as she neared the toilet.

Grace turned to Ewan as Walter went over to his bag of equipment to fiddle around with a small lens whilst quietly mumbling to himself. 'They seem like a friendly bunch.'

Ewan glanced at Walter before settling back on Grace, and she could see the warmth sitting there, just for her. That was something she recognised. 'They are, Grace. We all get on really well here.'

She took another couple of sips of her tea, then had to put the mug down, as Ewan's hands ruffling her scarf around her neck got in her way. He lowered his eyes, giving her the once over, then lightly tapped her nose with his index finger.

'You do look good, Gracie.'

So do you, Ewan. You always do. I can't believe we've not long broken up and we're still friends like this. Oh, wait. We haven't just broken up. That was years ago.

It was all so confusing. The way he was looking at her. The memory of feeling lucky to be with him, like she was the chosen one. But she wasn't. He chose many women. All whilst he was with her. She wasn't exclusive at all, and it didn't take long to stop feeling so lucky.

Look at you, standing there without a care in the world. Do you even know what you did to me? Do you even care?

She turned away, pretending to tidy the table just so she could take a moment to control her sigh.

As though reading her mind, Ewan walked around to face her. He raked one hand through his mop of brown hair, giving the impression he was nervous about something. 'Hey, Grace, I know we ended things on a bad note, but that was years ago, and we are great friends now. The best, in fact.' He dropped back to one heel, shortening his six-foot height as he breathed out a laugh. 'You know, it's funny how it's only the past four years you can't remember. It's as though your mind holds some sort of trauma it doesn't want to remember. At least I know that has nothing to do with me.'

What if my family are hiding it from me because they want the memory gone for my sake? What if...

'I don't mean to pry, Grace, but have things always been, how shall I put it, happy with Charlie? Does he treat you well? You know, he's the only one you can't remember.' Ewan shrugged into his coat as he turned away. 'I'm not saying he's a bad person. I'm just a bit worried he might be and that's why your mind is refusing to remember him.'

'I... I don't think he's a horrible person, Ewan. I...'

He reached out to her shoulder. 'It's okay, babe. I was stupid to ask. It's not like you would know anyway. Forget I mentioned it. I'm sure you're safe with him.'

Safe? Why did he use that word?

'Hey, Grace, do you remember that time we went horse riding and I kept wailing like a baby?' She slowly nodded. 'That was funny, wasn't it? Oh, and that day we spent our anniversary on the beach.' He pointed one finger at her chest. 'Jet skiing. Bloody brilliant. Aww, we had some laughs, you and me.' He lowered his head, then glanced up. 'I'm so sorry I messed things up between us. It was all my fault. I ruined everything.'

Grace stared silently down at her fingerless gloves as Ewan's hand slipped into hers.

'I miss so much about us, Gracie. You really were the only woman I loved.'

Grace watched his baby-blue eyes settle on her mouth, which caused her heart to flip, and she wasn't entirely sure if that was in a good way.

Please don't kiss me, Ewan. I don't know what I'd do if you do. I can't handle this right now.

It was true. They did have many lovely times together. But she was married. To Charlie. Who she didn't know, and now she was worried he had hurt her. What if his nice-guy image was just a front? He seemed nice, but Ewan was always nice too. In between cheating on her, controlling her, and causing her to walk on eggshells.

Did Charlie cheat? Was it worse than that? Why can't I remember Charlie? Ewan's right. There must be a reason my brain has omitted the years spent with my so-called husband.

A loud clap of the hands jolted Grace from her thoughts, and Ewan from staring at her lips.

'Right,' roared Veronica, entering the hall. 'Let's get this party started.' She practically gathered Grace up and marched her outside. 'We have a bit of a group party nearer Christmas. Just a few bevvies down The Ugly Duckling. You're in, eh, Grace?' She leaned closer, almost nudging Grace's ear with her nose. 'You can bring that beaut of a hubby with you. He's a nice man.'

Is he? I don't know anymore.

14

Charlie

Black Crow Alley in Sandly was flanked by old, narrow three-storey brown-brick food shops selling an array of artisan delicacies.

Charlie knew how much Grace loved to visit the place at Christmas. Everything was way more expensive than their local supermarket, so they only visited on special occasions.

Three steps with black wrought-iron banisters led up to the dark-oak door of every store, and witch-hat lamps poked out from walls in between each middle-floor iron balcony sheltering the doorways.

Charlie stood back a step, watching Grace's face twinkle with flecks of fairy lights from the three-foot, white-lit, real Christmas trees close to the black-framed shops along the alley. He glanced up at copper signs hanging from dark rods, filled with cursive shop names and established dates, then over at the building opposite with the ghost sign, revealing what once was long, long ago.

He turned his attention back to The Traditional Bakery, breathing in the aroma of freshly baked bread wafting out the opened door. Grace was peering in through the snow-sprayed Tudor bay window, deciding between the trays of different rolls she could see. He knew she would buy dark rye sourdough, as she always did.

She had been so quiet all morning. Since last night. And she'd kept her distance from him. She hadn't held his arm once and had hardly smiled his way, even when he mentioned their festive shopping spree.

Something's off. I can feel it. Or maybe she's just tired. Let's see how she feels after she's bought some of her favourite food.

He turned away from her to stare down the alley and laughed to himself at a memory that sprung to mind. 'Hey, Grace, you remember that time when... Oh, erm...' He frowned at himself as blue eyes flew his way with curiosity. He quickly flapped one hand. 'Never mind,' he mumbled.

'It's okay, Charlie. What were you going to say?'

Charlie didn't feel much like continuing with the memory, knowing full well it only belonged to him. He felt deflated and lonely, then annoyed for revealing signs about how he was feeling. Ever since Grace had come out of hospital, all he had tried to do was make her happy and comfortable. His feelings had to take a back seat. Sometimes, it was hard work holding everything inside.

'I just remembered that time we came here when it was foggy. We said it looked like a creepy London setting where we might see Sweeney Todd lurking in a doorway asking if anyone wants a shave.' He kept his tone as chirpy as possible, even though he knew it wasn't really working. If he could hear the breaks in his voice, surely she could too.

Grace looked over at Heritage Pie Shop and laughed. 'I can totally see that.'

Charlie gestured to the bakery. 'You wanna get something?' He waited outside whilst she popped in to buy some dark rye sourdough. There was only one other person in there, so he didn't wait long. It felt longer waiting for her to hold his arm. It felt even longer than that waiting for her to smile properly at him.

They mooched inside Mint Condition Herbs, gathering small pots of thyme and sage that Grace wanted to place on the kitchen windowsill. Charlie twiddled with a yellow-spotted plant pot, wishing he was as happy as they were last Christmas. He didn't know what to do about the plans they'd made for their future. It wasn't as though he could talk about them. They might not even have a future together anymore.

I'm losing her. I can feel her slipping away from me, and I don't know if I can save us.

He sniffed, keeping his back turned from Grace and the other shoppers. He could hear her engaged in friendly chatter with an assistant, acting as though life was normal. If only it were. He never realised how much of his life he took for granted. What life for him would look like without his wife. There wasn't one person on the planet he loved more than her. Today was the first day since he started dating her that he truly felt she had no love for him.

Grace nudged his arm, bringing him back to the present. 'You look deep in thought.'

Charlie held the plant pot forward. 'I was just wondering if you might like this one. It's pretty. What do you think?'

She lowered her eyes to look at the yellow pottery, and a sad smile emerged. 'I don't think you were contemplating herbs for the kitchen.'

He met her cautious gaze. 'Not now, Grace. This isn't the time or place.'

They paid for their goods, then stepped back outside into the alley. Charlie watched a waft of cold air leave his mouth and realised he had huffed loudly, earning him a worried glance from Grace. She nodded at the pizza restaurant, offering to buy lunch.

A warming aroma welcomed them inside Mama's Love, and a wood-fired mushroom and olive pizza gave them both genuine smiles for the first time that day, as its edges were decorated like a Christmas wreath, with coriander and some cherry tomatoes representing berries.

Charlie forced down his last mouthful, enjoying its flavours but not the atmosphere between them. There was more than the red-check dressed table dividing them. He stared at the dried candlewax down the sides of a green wine bottle, stopping just short of the fake holly sprigs entwined around its base, making the centrepiece. Grace's hand stretched across to his side, gaining his attention.

'Charlie, can you tell me something about our past?'

'What do you want to know?'

She hesitated, which rattled him a touch. 'I'm wondering if you and my family are hiding something from me.'

Charlie swallowed hard.

So, this is what her mood is about.

'Let's talk when we get home.'

'No, Charlie.' She pulled her hand back quickly before he had a chance to place his over her trembling fingers. Her voice was calm and low, but her eyes were fierce and demanding. She leaned closer, blocking out the other couple sitting over by the window. 'I don't want to spend the rest of my day wondering. Tell me now.'

He wanted to. Her whole family wanted her to know, but it wasn't a subject he felt could be tossed into a conversation. She was healing nicely, and he didn't want to put a spanner in the works.

Grace raised her eyebrows in annoyance. 'You have no right to keep things about my life from me. So, whatever it is, spit it out, or so help me, I'll up and leave, and you won't ever see me again.'

A whoosh of air fell out of his gut, cramping his stomach as though he had just been punched.

'Did you cheat on me, Charlie?'

'Whoa, whoa, whoa, what?' His eyes were wide, and his mouth even wider.

Tears formed in Grace's eyes, breaking his heart and ripping shreds out of his soul.

Her finger came up to wag across the table. 'Just tell me.'

He quickly grabbed it and lowered both their hands. 'Grace. No. Why would you think that?'

'It's not the first time it's happened to me.'

Charlie's shoulders tensed as he pulled his hand away and sat back. 'I'm not Ewan.'

'You're lying to me, just like he used to. So, yeah, right now, you are.'

Charlie jolted forward, trying hard not to cause a scene. 'I am nothing like him, and I will never be anything like him. Don't you put me in the same boat as him. I have not cheated on you.' He straightened and took a breath. 'Wait, is that what he told you last night? Did he say I cheated on you?' He looked around the room in a huff. 'I swear, I'm gonna kill him.'

'He didn't say that, okay. I'm asking you.'

'I don't wanna talk about our life in here.'

She stood, scraping her chair back, gaining attention from everyone inside.

Charlie was half out of his seat, showing her one palm. 'Whoa, whoa, okay, Grace. Sit down. I'll tell you.' He waved her back to her seat and breathed a relieved sigh as she sat.

'I'm not playing here, Charlie. If you've done something horrible to me in the past, I will find out. I'm not bloody stupid,' she whispered across the table.

He tapped at his chest, feeling wounded she would think that way about him. He just knew Ewan had something to do with this situation he was now facing. 'You need to stop thinking I'm a bad guy. I haven't done anything wrong.'

'You need to tell me the truth. And, yes, you have done something wrong. You did that the moment you made the decision to hide my life from me.' Her lips pursed and her fists tightened. 'What right have you got doing that, eh?'

Charlie leaned closer, moved the wine bottle out of his way, and reached forward to her hands clenched on her lap, refusing to meet his. 'Grace,' he said quietly. 'I'll tell you about the only hurt in our relationship, okay, but I'd rather not go into it in here.'

She folded her arms in a huff, showing him she wasn't about to go anywhere until he revealed what he was hiding from her.

Fine. Not how I wanted this to go down, but she's giving me no choice. Oh, this is just great. Right, okay, erm, how to say this...

He wiggled his fingers her way, asking her with his hands to come closer, but she wasn't budging. It wasn't very often Grace showed her stubborn side, but when she did, she won her battles. Charlie controlled his heart rate and tried again to encourage her to meet him in the middle of the table. She lowered her gaze and complied, much to his relief. 'Grace, let me hold your hand. Please.'

She faltered for a moment, then slowly released the tight grip on herself, reluctantly giving over one hand, which he huddled into his warm palms.

'Grace, honey, I love you with every beat of my heart. Never in a zillion years would I do anything to hurt you. You give me life. I need that to sink in. What we have is so special. It's something people spend years dreaming about. Wishing for. We got lucky. We found each other, and I'm not ready to lose you. You have to believe me when I tell you I would never hurt you.'

'What aren't you telling me?' Her voice was quiet and broken, almost pleading with him to be kind.

He swallowed hard, knowing she would spot that. He squeezed her hand ever so lightly. 'Last year, we lost a baby.' Her hand felt limp as her eyes dropped from his. 'It was hard for us, but we got through it as best we could. You were two months into your pregnancy, and we were excited. We had only just found out, then it was taken away from us all within a matter of two weeks. Erm, I don't know what else to add.'

Reliving the moment was just as hard as the actual time. Should he tell her they were going to try again next year? He wasn't sure what to say. She had made it perfectly clear she didn't appreciate him hiding things from her, but it felt wrong to mention future plans whilst they were so unstable.

Charlie raised her hand so he could kiss her knuckles. She looked so lost and taken aback, and there was little else he could do to comfort her whilst stuck in the middle of a pizza restaurant with the smell of garlic wafting up his nose every five minutes. He went to lower their hands, but she pulled them back up and returned his kiss, taking him by surprise.

'I'm sorry, Charlie.'

Without breaking their connection, he moved his chair around the table so he was right by her side. 'Hey, you have nothing to be sorry for.'

'I made you talk about something so sore when you didn't want to.'

He stroked the side of her hair and rested his head against hers. 'It's okay. I wanted to tell you, but I didn't know how to bring it up, that's all.'

'Yeah, I can see that now.' She moved her head so they could look at each other. 'So, we were trying for a baby?'

'We were giving it a go for a while back there.'

'And then we stopped?'

'We decided to have a break.'

She nodded slowly and sat back. 'Makes sense, I guess.'

He bent forward and kissed her cheek, whispering, 'I love you, Grace.'

'I don't know what to say, Charlie.'

'You don't have to say anything, honey.'

'Should we go home?'

'Sure, if that's what you want to do.' He followed her eyes over to the window.

'Not really. I'd like to stay here for a while. Get back to our day.'

'You know, we usually go over to the ice cream parlour and have gingerbread man ice cream with clotted cream. I kid you not.'

Grace smiled. 'Really? Wait, does that mean we normally come in here and have pizza for lunch too? Is this one of our traditions?'

Charlie raised one hand to get the waiter's attention so he could settle the bill. 'Yep, we're already set in our ways.' He gave her a cheeky wink as he handed over his debit card to pay. 'I was secretly smiling when you chose this place to eat. You see, Grace, it's still all there in you, tucked away somewhere, but there.'

The waiter gave back the card and walked away as Grace settled her hand on Charlie's thigh.

'Do you think I can't remember my time with you because of the trauma of losing a baby?'

'I don't know, Grace, but now you do know, is it triggering anything?'

She shook her head as she stood to put on her coat. 'No. Sorry.'

He handed over her scarf, then wrapped his own. 'It's okay.' He paused to watch her as she got herself ready for the cold. 'Are we good now, Grace?' He could feel his heart hanging on for dear life.

Gentle blue eyes smiled softly up at him. 'I do believe you love me, but I'm still finding my feet here, okay?'

He pulled in his lips, nodded, and smiled. 'Okay.'

15

Grace

After shovelling down the last mini gingerbread man from her dollop of ginger-infused ice cream, Grace clutched at her stomach. 'I seriously cannot eat another morsel.' She nodded at her empty plate. 'I blame the clotted cream.'

'Oh, yeah, blame that after seven gingerbread men.' Charlie laughed as he sipped on diet cola.

'Hey, they're teeny-tiny ones. Please tell me we normally buy a box to take home.' She watched his gorgeous smile fill his face, loving how alight his features became whenever he was happy. She had grown quite accustomed to the warm glow his face emitted.

She wondered if he'd got over the fact she accused him of being a cheater. She couldn't believe she'd forced him to tell her such sad news in a pizza restaurant. She remembered her mum telling her about when she lost her own baby, in between Molly and Harriet. She said it wasn't anyone's fault. It was just one of those things that happens and nobody knows why.

I guess that makes me a mum now, even if my baby's not with me. I love you, my baby, wherever you are. This is so surreal.

She glanced over at Charlie as something inside her resembling love stirred. He caught her looking and flashed a smile that warmed her heart.

'Hey, Charlie, I have an idea.'

'If it's anything to do with gingerbread men, count me in.'

She breathed out a laugh whilst shaking her head. 'No. Well, it could include a box. Listen, last night, Ashley told me they're having a Christmas Eve party up at the castle. So, I was thinking, what if we set up a food hamper and raffle it off at the party and the proceeds go to the Donkey Sanctuary? We're always looking for ways to bring in more money. While we're here, we could go around each shop and ask them to donate some of their lovely artisan food to the hamper.'

A flash of a large wicker basket whizzed in and out of her mind so fast, she wasn't quite sure if she was seeing things. 'Charlie, by any chance do we have an old hamper basket in the loft?'

His eyes widened in surprise. 'We do.'

'I think I just remembered that. I'm not sure.'

Charlie lowered his drink and clasped his hands. 'We'll take it, Grace. Whatever comes to mind, we'll take it as a win.'

'Well, okay, but it's rather an odd thing to remember, don't you think?'

Charlie raised his palms and breathed out a laugh. 'This whole thing is odd, but we'll take what we're given. No stress, no force. Let's go back to talking hampers. Maybe raising funds for where you work is a trigger. It's something you've always been highly involved in. It's a passion, so it could be sparking something.'

'Okay. So, we'll ask the lady at the counter if she has any boxes out back, then we'll have something to carry all the goods in. Ooh, perhaps some of the shops can donate gift tokens for the new year. I can't see bread lasting very long in a hamper, so we can ask at the bakery for something like that, and maybe a meal for two at Mama's Love. Although,

I'm not sure I want to go back in there now. I'm pretty sure they were all watching us.'

'Hey, don't worry about them. We'll go back, ask, and leave. This is a great idea, honey. I'm totally on board and raring to go. So, let's see, what have we got down here?'

'We can ask for some gingerbread men here. That's a start. Then we can get some oils and vinegars, ooh, and some jam and chutney.'

'What about a voucher from The Fat Hog. We're going there for some honey-roasted cured ham anyway.'

'I love that stuff.'

'Yeah, I know. We usually buy some for your parents too.'

Grace felt a flush of warmth fill her again. The feeling really was becoming a very good friend. One she would happily invite around anytime for a cuppa. 'My dad used to buy some really good ham every Christmas. That and walnuts. He's always had a thing for walnuts this time of year.'

'We always end our trip here with a packet of roasted chestnuts. There's a man with a stall at the end of the alley, and we're loyal Christmas customers.'

'Mmm, I can taste them already.'

Charlie pointed over at her stomach and grinned. 'You said you had no more room.'

'I will by the time we're finished collecting hamper donations.'

They both laughed, and Grace pulled out her phone to send Ashley a text, letting her know about the raffle plan.

'Hey, Grace, will you be my date for the Christmas Eve party?' His words were so soft and sexy, her heart did a flip more glorious than a dolphin playing in the waves of a sunsetting ocean.

It took her a moment to realise she was twiddling her hands on her lap and grinning from ear to ear, looking like a bashful schoolgirl just been asked to prom by the best-looking boy in town.

He is the best-looking boy in town, and he's my husband. And, my goodness, does he look hot right now. He has very good cheekbones. I bet he's really photogenic.

Before she questioned her actions, she quickly snapped a shot of him using her phone.

The corners of his mouth twitched. 'What was that? You capturing the moment I asked you to the most exclusive party of the year?'

'Ha! No, it's just your face.'

'What about it?' He touched his cheek, looking half chuffed and half worried.

'I like it.'

Charlie's eyes twinkled as his face relaxed into an easy smile. 'I like yours too.'

Grace put her phone in her handbag and gave him her best innocent look. 'And, yes, I will go to the party with you, Dr Wallis.'

He slapped one hand over his heart dramatically with mock relief. 'Phew! That was a stressful few seconds. I thought you were going to leave me hanging.' He leaned his elbow on the white table, turning his head on his knuckles. 'So, I'll pick you up at seven. Say, in the hallway?'

Grace naturally gravitated towards him. 'It's a date.'

His sexy smile broadened, causing wave after wave of adrenaline to smack into her diaphragm. 'It sure is.'

She had to break free from the spell she was under, locked with his midnight eyes, so she slapped his arm, causing him to jolt upright. 'Come on, let's get mingling with the locals. I need to get my salesperson hat on.'

'Salesperson? I thought you were the one buying.'

'Not buying, Charlie. Selling the Donkey Sanctuary's needs, wants, and desires. I can have the hardest of folk crying into their cloves of garlic and spiced-rum conserves by the time I'm finished with my save-the-donkey plea.'

'Oh, I believe you.'

'You know, if this goes well, we could get more hampers. What about a Pepper Lane one as well as our Black Crow Alley one?'

Charlie nodded as he stacked their empty plates and moved them to one side with the glasses, making the table neat and tidy. 'Sounds like a plan.'

'Ooh, and what about one filled with treatments like a haircut, shave, massage, and other beauty bits and bobs? There are loads of independent shops in the town centre, and I know a lot of the owners.' She reached out and grabbed his hands fussing over the scrunched paper napkins between them. 'We can raise a lot of money. I feel so excited about this.'

'No, really? I never would have guessed. Your bouncing eyeballs didn't give that away at all.'

She tightened her lips. 'My eyeballs do not bounce.'

'They totally do.'

She lightly tapped his hands. 'Be serious. Oh, this is going to be so much fun. Wait till I tell Red. Ooh, and we'll have to stop off at the stationery shop and buy some raffle tickets.'

'Erm, let's just see what we can get out of the shopkeepers first.'

Grace flapped one hand his way. 'Oh, please, they'll be putty in my hand. I'll get something from all of them, just you wait and see.'

Charlie leaned back in his chair and beamed a satisfied smile. 'It's good to see you again, Grace Hadley.'

This is what I need. Normality. Being the person I know I am, instead of trying to figure out who I'm supposed to be. I can raise money for the donkeys in my sleep.

She stood, glancing over at the cold counter filled with an array of colourful ice cream. 'It's Grace Wallis, I'll have you know. And, yes, I'm back.'

Charlie leapt from his chair, cupped his hands around her face, and tenderly kissed her on the mouth. 'I couldn't resist.'

Grace felt flustered. 'Well, I... erm, just so you know, it... it felt quite nice.'

Quite nice? That's an understatement. Flipping heck, I can't feel my legs. Okay, woman, get a grip.

'Erm, I'll just go ask that lady for a box.' She glanced back, tripping over her own foot as she watched Charlie smiling to himself whilst gathering plates as though he worked in Ice Cream, We All Scream.

The young lady happily went out the back to see if they had any boxes they could use, and Grace waited by the counter, staring over at Charlie.

Oh goodness, I want to rip his clothes off and cover him in tutti-frutti. Then, I can lick it off and... Crap, he's seen me. I swear he just read my mind.

Grace swallowed hard and was pleased to have the distraction of the woman returning with two large white boxes.

The shop assistant swished her long, green-tipped ponytail away from her shoulder. 'My boss said you can have a box of gingerbread men to start you off too. He's mates with Red, from their schooldays, so he's happy to help. I think he wants you to mention that fact to her.' She offered a wink along with the goods, and Grace winked back.

123

Charlie approached, handing over the plates and glasses, earning him a fluttering of eyelashes and the shine of a fixed brace from the widest smile the young woman could offer.

Ha! Get your own, lady. This one's taken. Oh, look at Charlie. Big goof. Does he even notice stuff like this? Hot Doc isn't even fazed. Let's see if this rattles him.

Grace moved her hand slowly down and placed it upon his lower back, with the tips of her fingers resting just upon his bum. And there, she caught a shift in his eyes, even though they weren't looking her way. Her experiment was unexpected, and she was so pleased she had caught him off guard. His Adam's apple bobbed, his body tensed, and then the most darkened of eyes dominated the whole shop as his head slowly turned her way.

It was Grace's turn to swallow hard and stiffen. Her eyes were suddenly locked into some sort of magical hold she couldn't escape from, not that she wanted to, but they were being watched by a twenty-something shop assistant, so something had to give.

Without removing his eyes, Charlie took the boxes from the young woman and said his thanks.

Finally, he broke contact, and Grace managed to gulp some cool, sweet-scented air as she removed the box of gingerbread men from the gawping woman, who also looked transfixed as though under a love spell.

'Grace,' called Charlie from the doorway, breaking her trance-like state and making her jump slightly.

'Hmm? Yes, coming.'

Their eyes met again as he opened the door with one hand whilst balancing the boxes with the other. He leaned closer to her ear as she slowly passed him by.

'Grace, I wanna cover you in tutti-frutti right now, then clean it all off with my tongue.'

Oh my...

She stumbled, nearly falling down the steps, but Charlie's hand shot out and caught her arm, and the electricity that flowed through her was enough to bring the whole island alive with Christmas lights.

The smallest of tugs hit the corner of Charlie's lips. 'Best not to touch me in certain places when we have company, eh, Grace?'

Noted. But, my goodness, I want to do it again.

It was Grace's turn to curl one corner of her mouth. She waited until he had hold of the boxes in both hands, and then, with defiant eyes locked with his, she stroked one hand over his bum.

'Right!' He dropped the boxes, and Grace let out a small scream and quickly jumped the stairs, showing him her palms.

'Charlie, no.' She placed one hand over her mouth to muffle the giggle escaping.

His smiling eyes narrowed as he groaned. 'I'm not picking up these boxes until you promise to behave.' He glanced down at them by his feet. 'Unless you want to carry them and have your hands restricted.'

Grace was still muffling her laughter. 'Okay, okay. I promise.'

His eyes narrowed even more, then he bent to retrieve the boxes and made his way down the steps to offer out his elbow.

Grace latched on to his arm and nudged his shoulder with her head. 'You have a very nice bum, Dr Wallis.'

He turned and the tip of his nose nuzzled into her woolly hat. 'Yours is even better. Especially smeared with whipped cream.'

Grace's cheeks heated as she snorted out a laugh.

Charlie's nose nudged the bottom of her earlobe. 'Oh, honey, I'm not joking. We have totally been there.'

She turned to meet his eyes, and in her best sultry voice, she asked, 'Did I taste good?'

The boxes he held wobbled for less than a second, then those midnight eyes of his turned to total eclipse. He tilted his head and breathed out a small cloud of cold air as his lips parted. 'Oh, Gracie, I can still taste you now.'

16

Charlie

After spending the day watching Grace working her charm on shopkeepers, telling her about the miscarriage, having her touch his backside, and seeing her face full of life, Charlie was taking long, deep breaths as he stood under the hot water of his shower. It wasn't even dinner time and he felt more washed-out than the cubicle.

Oh jeez, what a day.

He lowered his face, allowing the heat to consume him as steam hid his tight forehead muscles.

'Charlie?'

A spray of water hit him straight in the eyes as his head shot up from the beige-tiled floor. He turned to see if Grace could see him naked through the screen.

'Grace?' He cuffed away the dollop of water that had landed in his mouth. 'Is everything okay?' He could make out movement heading towards the toilet.

'Yeah, I just…'

He couldn't see her through the steam, and her voice was barely audible. 'What was that?' He placed one hand on the glass divide of the shower and leaned around its curve to see her sitting on the closed toilet seat. Wiping his hand down his face, he widened his eyes and blinked a couple of times. 'You okay, Grace?'

Her eyes were on the pink dressing gown belt she was twiddling on her lap. 'I was just waiting to jump in the shower.'

'Oh, erm, right. I won't be a sec.' He went to turn back to quickly shampoo his hair, but she called his name again. Meeting her eyes this time, he could instantly tell she wanted to talk about more than her evening shower.

Grace stood, sighed deeply, then let her robe fall to a slump at her feet, revealing her naked body along with a slightly awkward stance.

Oh my God.

Any other time, he wouldn't be standing there gawping like a dumbstruck idiot.

Come on, Charlie, get it together, man. That's your wife standing there, obviously wanting you. What you gonna do about it?

'Erm, Grace, honey, I… What… Umm.'

Shit, I don't know what to say.

'Charlie, can I get in the shower with you?'

He knew his eyes had just widened, because he could feel the stretch of his brow. Under normal circumstances, he would have himself wrapped up in her by now, and she wouldn't be standing there looking nervous, having to ask. He swallowed hard, desperately trying to form words that made sense and fitted their unusual situation and, in his case, unexpected situation.

'Grace, erm…' He wiped his face again, and her eyes left him to look sullenly down at her robe. Suddenly, he felt like crap because he could see she felt rejected, and that wasn't something he had ever done to her. 'Sure,' he added quickly, giving her a wave of the hand towards him.

She hesitated, clearly deciding between the dressing gown and shower. Charlie was taking full blame for that indecision. Grace had obviously built up a whole heap of courage to come at him with nakedness and steamy shower scenes.

'Grace.' He spoke softly and held out his hand. 'It's okay, honey.' He wriggled his fingers, and she smiled slightly at the pruned tips. Charlie kissed her knuckles as she placed her hand in his, before entering the shower.

She glanced over her shoulder as she stood between him and the showerhead. 'I assume we've done this before.'

It was so hard not to kiss her neck, shoulder, back, all down her body. His eyes wandered all over her as he held himself back from touching her skin.

'Yes, we've done this plenty of times.'

Not quite like this, but let's not go there.

Charlie stretched his neck, looking up at the ceiling, trying to think of how to handle the moment. He was practically a stranger to her, yet there they were, naked in the shower, and both acting as though it were their first time seeing each other that way.

Sure as hell feels like the first time. I think I was less nervous back then.

'Charlie, will you touch me?'

He gaped whilst staring at her back. He quickly pulled himself together as she turned to face him. 'Grace, I…'

One of her hands rested over his heart, causing it to stop long enough for him to feel a tad lightheaded. 'I know you've probably touched me loads of times, but I want to know what it feels like to have your hands move over my body.'

The thought alone caused his breath to catch. He was having one hell of a battle with himself, as never before had his wife had to ask him to touch her.

'Grace, I don't want to take advantage of you.' He lowered his hands that were about to rest on her shoulders and slip down her arms and tug at her hips. He placed them behind his back, removing all temptation.

Her head tilted to one side as her eyes narrowed with confusion. 'Why do you think that?'

'Because you hardly know me, and I want to make love to you when you do.'

'What if I never remember you? Will you never touch me again?'

'I—'

'We flirted today. I thought you wanted me.'

A breath of anxiety huffed out his mouth. He took a step closer and let go of the grip he had on his hands behind his back. 'Oh, I want you. So much. You have no idea how much this is killing me right now.'

'So do something about it. I want to know what my husband feels like.'

His eyes left hers for a moment to scan his feet. 'Grace…' His voice cracked, so he swallowed hard and tried again. Raising his gaze, he could see hurt and stubbornness facing him. Words were struggling to free themselves from his mouth, and his hands were starting to fidget close to his thighs. He went to speak, but Grace grabbed his head and forced her lips onto his, taking his breath away altogether. She slammed him back to the brown tiles, pinning him in place with her body.

It took Charlie all of three seconds to regain control of his whirling head. He kissed her back with everything he had to offer, clashing teeth whilst desperately caressing her tongue. As they came up for air, he swiftly lifted her and turned around so it was her back up against the wall. She wrapped her legs around him as his mouth explored the length of her neck.

'Grace,' he mumbled onto her warm skin. 'Oh God, Grace.'

I have to stop. This isn't right. I can't do this. Not now. She has to know me. She has to. It can't be this way.

He removed his mouth and gently placed her back down, taking a moment before stepping back and lowering his head in defeat. 'I can't.'

One of her fingers came up to stroke over his lips. 'How long were we together before we had sex for the first time?'

He met her eyes, knowing she would chastise him as soon as she found out. 'Three weeks.'

As expected, her eyebrows lifted and her mouth hung loose. 'So, we knew each other such a short time and we connected in this way.' She scanned his dripping wet body, and he had no choice but to nod. 'And yet, here we are now, and you won't be with me.'

Charlie scrunched his eyes tightly for a moment as he drew breath. 'It's not the same, Grace. Come on, you know how things are. I just don't want to do this with you while you're confused.'

She poked his chest in annoyance. 'Don't tell me how I feel.' She slumped back against the wall as she mumbled loud enough to be heard over the falling water. 'It's not your place to tell me about myself.'

'I'm sorry.'

Defiant eyes glared his way. 'I'm sick to death with being told about myself. I know me. I know me.' She slapped away at her collarbone, splashing out spits of hot water.

'I'm sorry.'

'No, you don't get to be sorry.' Her voice grew strong and aggravated as she straightened and stepped closer to him. 'This is my life. Mine. And I'll do what I want with my husband, do you hear me. You're my husband, and if I want to make love, you have to want me. Why are you making excuses?' He went to answer but she wasn't finished. 'I'm standing here naked in front of you, wanting you, needing you, asking you to make all the bad stuff go away, but you won't help me.' Tears streamed from her eyes, meeting the shower water on her chest. 'You're supposed to be the one I can turn to, the one who is there for me, but you're not here with me, are you? I need to get all this crap out of my mind.'

Charlie reached out to pull her towards him, but she slapped him away.

'No. Don't touch me.' She placed a hand over her mouth as though trying hard to hold in the weighted air forcing itself from her lungs. 'I lost a baby. A baby, Charlie, and I can't remember, but it hurts.' She whacked his chest, causing him to jolt, but he didn't move. 'It hurts. It hurts so much.' Her tears were coming faster, and her breathing was shaky and catching every other second. 'Charlie, I... I...'

He caught her in his arms before her body could meet the floor. Each strangled cry tore another piece of his heart as his own tears met her drenched hair.

'Charlie.' She sobbed out his name over and over until her words faded into the steam.

'It's okay, Grace. I've got you. I've got you, honey. It's going to be okay.' He lifted her into his arms and carried her out of the shower, leaving it running. Large brown towels were folded neatly in a pile upon a wooden shelf. He swiped the top one and quickly sat on the bath mat whilst draping the bath towel over them both. He reached up to grab another to place over her wet hair, where he gently swirled his hand in an attempt to dry her so she didn't feel cold.

Grace's body felt frail and was slowly settling in his hold. He lowered his mouth to her covered head and rested his lips there for a moment as she sniffed and cleared her throat.

'I'm sorry.' Her words were muffled and broken.

He used his nose to nudge the top of the towel covering her hair. 'Hey, hey, you have nothing to be sorry for.'

The towel fell lopsided on her face as she moved her head to gaze up at him. 'I tried so hard to put it out of my mind today. I didn't want to think about us losing a baby. I thought, if I concentrated on raising money instead, it would quietly go away, but it didn't, so I came in here to find you. I just wanted you to make it go away.' She dipped her head again as more tears fell.

Charlie wrapped her tightly in his arms, stroking one hand in circles over her back whilst whispering out a shushing noise close to her ear.

'I'm sorry, Charlie,' she said quietly.

'It's okay, honey. I knew it would hit you at some point. It's a lot to take in. We've had quite a day, huh? It's okay. You're gonna be just fine, I promise. I've got you.'

'Have you really got me?'

'Yeah, I've got you. Always.'

The noise of the running water filled the air for a few minutes, sounding like rain against the window, and a hint of mango shower gel lingered in amongst the steam as though adding in remnants of a tropical storm.

'I'm sorry I made it all about sex and donkeys.'

Charlie raised his brow in amusement as he stared over at the shower. 'Now there's a sentence I never thought I'd hear.'

A muffled laugh came from beneath the crumpled towels followed by a snort, a sniff, and then a hand that wriggled free to land on his shoulder. Charlie scrunched up his side so he could place a light kiss on her fingertips, tasting her salty tears and damp skin.

'Thanks, Charlie.' Grace's voice was barely a whisper as her hand gave one stroke of his neck. 'For being here for me.'

'I'll never be anywhere else, Grace. I love you. So, what I'm thinking now is, we get back in that shower, wash your hair properly, then PJs and food. What do you say to takeout?'

'Food sounds good.'

'Then, that's that sorted.'

Grace wriggled on his lap until she was sitting up facing him, bleary eyes and all. He met her with a warm smile and playfully nudged her nose with his own, and it warmed his heart to see her smile with what looked very much like love in her flushed face.

'Charlie, I was thinking, we could invite Harrison to eat with us. He must miss Ashley at night. We can treat them to dinner and tell them both thanks, and then, well, how would you feel if I tell my sister she can go home?'

'You ready for that?'

Her damp hair stuck to her cheek as she nodded and smiled. 'I am. Are you?'

He reached out to remove the strands of hair from her face as he nodded. 'I am.'

'Okay then.'

Charlie twiddled the damp locks around his finger, watching his own slow movements, transfixed with touching her. 'Ready for the shower again?'

She scrambled off his lap and held out her hand to help tug his cramped legs from the floor. 'Yes. Let's get on with it. I'm looking forward to dinner now it's been mentioned.'

He let her lead him back beneath the hot water, all the while smiling to himself at how relaxed and calm she was now.

Ah, man, we really needed that breakthrough. I'm so glad she's doing okay now, and she trusts me. She actually trusts me. This is going to be okay. Just keep holding on. And breathe.

He watched her shampoo her hair whilst talking about how Harrison and Ashley could help make up some of the hampers with them after dinner, and all he could think about was how much love he held inside his heart for her and how fragile that made him feel.

17

Grace

Grace and Ashley stood inside Doll's Gift House, seeing what gifts Dolly would donate to their hamper from her shop in Pepper Lane. Whilst she was out the back sorting out her handmade candles, Ashley asked Grace if she was one hundred percent sure she was happy with being alone with Charlie.

'It'll be your first time tonight, Gracie.'

'It would have been my first night alone with him last night if you had just gone back with Harrison after dinner, like I told you to.'

Ashley shrugged whilst swooshing the tip of her braid over her lips. 'I needed to gather my stuff, Grace. You can't just kick a person out like that.'

Grace raised her eyebrows in amusement. 'Really? Kick you out. You had one overnight bag, Ash. I knew you were worried. You're still worried. Admit it.'

'I just want to be sure, that's all. It's a big step.'

'I told Charlie in the beginning I was going to give us a go, and I feel as if I can't do that properly with you there every night. I have to try for some sort of normality.'

Ashley gave her a knowing look. 'Have you told Mum yet?'

Grace dipped her head and made her way over to the window to stare outside at the cold view of Pepper Lane. Some white lights were strung up high, crossing over from shop to shop on either side of the quiet road, and someone had thrown red tinsel over the small wall by the shingle beach at the bottom of the slanted road.

Ashley moved to her side, nudging her arm. 'You know she won't like it, Grace, but don't worry. I'll have a word.'

'It's okay, Ash. I need to do this myself. Mum can't keep treating me like a kid. I know she's worried about me, that's understandable, but I have to try and get back to my life.'

'How are things with you and Charlie at the moment?'

Grace scrunched one shoulder up to her ear. She wasn't quite sure how to answer, as she wasn't quite sure what kind of relationship they had. Everything felt up and down, and most days she was confused and unsure of everything, but then there were the moments where so much felt so right. His smile, his laughter, the look in his eyes when they turned her way. Something about him made every part of her want to know every part of him.

Ashley bumping her arm brought her thoughts to a halt. 'Has anything returned yet, Grace? Anything at all?'

'Sometimes things feel familiar, but I second-guess every thought and feeling. If I think too hard, it gives me headache, then I feel tired. I'm trying out the not thinking approach, but when you try to not think, you think even more.'

'You've got counselling tomorrow. Are you going to go?'

Grace turned to face her sister and reluctantly nodded. 'I'm going to give it a try. I don't feel it's for me, but Charlie says I need to go. I'm not sure if that's just him being a doctor, but he seems to be sitting firm with this one.'

'I'm not the type to go in for all that either, but it's worth a try. You never know, it might help settle your mind. Plus, Harrison says you learn coping techniques, so that could be helpful. He's been going for years, ever since he had to have his first operation. He almost lost half his face. That's not a trauma that's going to just bugger off because a certain number of years have passed. Grace, you have to forget about timing too, and just take each day as it comes.'

'Yeah, I know. And when I think about Harrison, it makes me remember there are people far worse off than me.'

'Hey, he's not far worse off than anyone. Don't let him hear you say that. Harrison has a good life, and he's happy. And anyway, it doesn't matter if someone else has a brain tumour and you have a migraine, it doesn't take away the fact you're suffering. Don't compare. But you can learn from others. Speak to Harrison. See how he copes with the bad days. Maybe he'll have some tips for you.'

'Yeah, I might just do that. But I'll also see what the therapist has to say tomorrow. I'm reading my diary too, so catching up with my past that way. I really got into the photography thing, and I still like taking pictures, and Charlie said I was going to turn a room into a studio, but, Ash, truthfully, I'm not feeling it.'

Ashley flapped one hand. 'That's okay. Just do whatever feels right. Whatever makes you happy. Don't be forced into anything just because that's the way it used to be. Your life is like the new year. You get to start afresh. If you want to make new plans, go for it, I say.'

'I kind of like what we're doing now. I love the Donkey Sanctuary so much. I feel myself come alive whenever I think about it, and raising money to help keep it ticking over is really making me feel as though I fit in a place I don't have to try and squeeze myself into.'

Ashley started to flick through some tea towels piled on a table by the door. 'That's probably because you've always worked there. You're the one who always raises money for that place. They'd be lost without you. Red should have given you a raise years ago. She's so tight.'

The shop owner came out from the back, holding two scented candles wrapped in cellophane and red bows. 'How about these ones?' Dolly placed them on the counter, smiling proudly at her work. 'Cinnamon and apple spice.'

Grace picked one up to inhale the Christmassy aroma. 'Hmm, thank you. These will look so good in the Pepper Lane hamper, especially since we mostly have vouchers for this one.'

Dolly rolled her big chestnut eyes over to the window. 'Pop over to The Book Gallery. Scott's over there now. He'll find a nice print to add to the basket. It'll be one of his own, so no skin off anyone's nose. Although Anna will probably toss in a book or two.'

Grace glanced over her shoulder at the doorway. 'Ooh, do you mean Scott Harper? Is he back in town?'

Ashley chuckled as she gestured towards Dolly. 'Yeah, Grace. This is his partner, Dolly Lynch. They live up at Lemon Drop Cottage.'

'Blimey, what else don't I know?'

'Dolly's from Ireland, but then moved to Hastings, and then here.'

Grace twisted her mouth to one side as she tilted her head towards her sister. 'You don't need to tell me she's from Ireland, Ash. I think I worked that much out by her accent.'

Dolly giggled. 'It's a dead giveaway.'

Grace smiled her way. 'Well, I'm glad you've found a home here, which should mean you know all the local gossip by now. So, Dolly, hit me. What else don't I know?'

Dolly leaned her elbows on the counter, beckoning her two customers closer. 'Well, Tessie Sparrow married Nate Walker, not sure if you know that, and Anna is Jake Reynolds' wife. They met on his rooftop in London. She was living in a tent there, would you believe.'

Grace pointed at the ceiling, to where her sister lived in the flat above. 'Yeah, Molly told me about them, but no one mentioned Tessie got married. Nate Walker, eh?' She nodded to herself whilst biting her bottom lip. 'Makes sense, I guess.' She turned back to Dolly. 'So, have we already met?'

Dolly smiled warmly as she nodded. 'Once or twice. Scott first introduced me to you and your husband when we saw you in the restaurant over at Pepper River Inn.'

'Oh, you mean The Inn on the Left?'

Ashley nodded whilst examining one of the candles. 'Yeah, but it's got its original name back now. The two hotels rejoined.'

Grace folded her arms and exhaled deeply. 'So much has happened over the last few years. I can't believe how much has changed.'

Dolly scrunched her nose as she gave a slight nod. 'I think a lot changes in one day, but we don't always notice. People tend to count the years rather than the moments.'

Charlie's surprised face flashed through her mind. He was entering the Santa photo booth at the Sandly Christmas Market. She wasn't sure if that was a memory or the visual was there because she'd been told about it.

Oh, this is so annoying. I'm sure I just remembered that. There was that red and brown scarf he had on and the silly reindeer antlers, and, my goodness, was he super-cute.

Her eyebrows tightened, so she relaxed her face by wiping away the thought, which wasn't her favourite technique, but she found it easy to handle.

Ashley and Dolly were still catching her up on any events she might have missed, when the door opened and Ewan poked his head inside.

'Hello, Grace. Thought that was you in here.'

Grace turned from the women to go over to the doorway to greet him, but not before catching a look of distaste hit her sister's eyes. 'Ewan, I was hoping to see you at some point.'

'Oh, missing me already?'

She breathed out a laugh that she hoped didn't sound rude. She wasn't really feeling any animosity towards him, but she also wasn't feeling as though she needed to be his friend. 'I just wanted to let the group know I won't be coming back again. I'll meet them down the pub for a Christmas drink, that's still on, but I'm not feeling the photography right now.'

He looked sad, then his expression switched to annoyance. 'Is this because of Chas?'

'Charlie, and no. I just need to concentrate on rebuilding my life.'

'Photography is a big part of your life now.' He flapped one hand up towards his shoulder. 'You took school pictures, for crying out loud. You were getting jobs. You're good at it. I don't think you should be too quick to drop the lot.'

Grace glanced over her shoulder to see Ashley had disappeared out the back with Dolly. She controlled the huff wanting to leave her mouth and turned back to Ewan. 'I understand that, but I feel more at home with the donkeys.'

'That's fair enough. You're a big part of the place, but you're more than that, babe. You were starting to become a somebody around here. Surely you don't want to go back to having no career.'

'I just want to do what makes me feel comfortable and happy.'

Ewan's whole face revealed he wasn't agreeing with that statement. He reached out to hold her by the elbows. 'Grace, I don't know what people are filling your head with, but I'm telling you the truth. You loved being a photographer more than anything. If you don't believe me, ask anyone in our group. Please don't throw it all away.'

'Well, maybe I'll think some more about it in the new year, but right now, I just need to focus on my charity work, getting through Christmas, and living with my husband on my own again.'

Ewan's brow lifted. 'Yeah, how's that going?'

Grace could tell he didn't like Charlie. It wasn't as though Ewan was hiding the fact. She wriggled out of his hold and scratched at her neck, loosening her scarf, as a flush of heat was irritating her skin. 'Ashley's moving out today, so I guess I'll have to see how it goes.'

Ewan scoffed quietly and rolled his eyes. 'I bet that wasn't the dentist's idea.'

'Doctor, and no, it was mine actually. Why did you say it like that?'

Ewan lowered his eyes, shuffled his feet, and then looked up and gently tapped her arm with his fist. 'Well, you know.'

'No, I don't know.'

Ewan gestured towards the back room. 'Him and Ashley.'

Grace stepped closer and kept her voice as low as his. 'What about them?'

Ewan stepped back, rubbing one hand over his stubble. 'Ah, Grace, come on. I don't like to say if no one has mentioned it to you.'

'Well, you had better tell me now you've brought it up.' Grace's heart was pumping, her hands shaking, and her soul was getting ready to up and leave her numbing body behind.

He didn't speak or even move, so she poked him in his coat's breast pocket.

'Bloody well tell me, Ewan,' she said through clenched teeth. 'What about Charlie and Ashley?'

He lowered his head so his face was inches from hers. 'No one's a hundred percent sure, but by the way he looks at her when he thinks no one is looking, well, babe, it doesn't exactly look good, you know.'

Grace was feeling more and more flustered by the second.

'What do you mean? How does he look at her?'

I've not noticed anything. Has Charlie been giving my sister long, lustful glances? Does Ashley know? Does Harrison?

Ewan arched his right eyebrow. 'Come on, Grace. Don't make me be the one who has to spell it out for you.' Before she could say anything, he quickly added, 'There are rumours about the two of them. Some people think they've been together behind your back.' He straightened and raised his voice slightly. 'Not me, of course, and I shut them down as soon as I hear anyone gossiping about your life.' He reached out and placed a strand of her hair behind her ear that didn't need moving. 'You know I think the world of you, Grace. I would never do anything to add to the hurt I caused you. For the last four years, all I've ever done was find ways to make it up to you, so there's no way I'd be party to any of that. I always stick up for you.'

'Why would you need to stick up for me?'

'You know.' He tilted his head, giving her a sympathetic smile. 'Because they say you're a mug.'

The only person who mugged me off was you. Oh, bloody hell, is Charlie doing it to me too? And Ashley?

Grace was wracking her brain, trying to think back to every look Charlie gave Ashley. Was she missing something? Anything? She just couldn't be sure. Her headache had returned and brought with it a churning in her gut that swirled and whirled, causing nausea and twinges of cramp.

'I'm sorry, babe. I thought someone would have mentioned it to you by now. I did think it was a bit strange when I heard Ash was living with you two.' He breathed out a long sigh and rested his hand on her shoulder. 'Still, look on the bright side. At least she's going now. That will probably help your relationship with Chucky.'

'Charlie,' she whispered, just about managing that.

18

Charlie

Grace's whole family were at Waterside Cottage, packing hampers and toy boxes, cooking dinner and baking cookies, pouring drinks and swapping Christmas presents, filling the place with festive cheer and noise. A lot of noise.

Charlie was in the kitchen getting more of a headache from Fiona, who was annoyed that Ashley was moving out. He could understand her concern, but it didn't stop him feeling like some sort of monster who couldn't be trusted. Ever since he met Grace's family, he had got on with them all, but now they were making him feel like an outsider. One who didn't know Grace Hadley at all. And it hurt. It hurt like hell, but there he was, putting on his brave face and best smile, using his bedside manner and dealing-with-upset-family-members techniques. Everything he was feeling had to be pushed to the back burner once again. Grace's well-being came first. He just needed Fiona to step back and let them both breathe.

'Mum, Grace will be fine,' snapped Ashley, removing almost-burnt star cookies from the oven.

Fiona slumped down at the table, picking up a glass of Buck's Fizz. 'Well, she doesn't look that great to me, Ashley. In fact, she's ever so quiet tonight, and that's not my Grace.' She glanced up at Charlie. 'If any of my girls go quiet, I know something is wrong. It's just not normal. With the exception of our Lexi, that is. She's always in her own head, is that one. When she's quiet, she's talking to characters in her mind. Always best not to interrupt.'

Charlie turned to meet Ashley's concerned eyes. 'Fiona has a point, Ash. Grace has been pretty quiet since you two got back.'

'Yeah, she was all right this morning. Happy as anything, talking donkeys and Christmas. You know, her two favourite subjects. And then, I don't know, she just changed.'

Fiona swallowed her drink whole, then turned back to Charlie, waving her glass for him to refill. 'How many ups and downs has she been having?'

'A few.' He didn't want to lie. 'But that's to be expected. It's perfectly normal for anyone who has been through such a trauma to experience high and low periods while in recovery. And she is still recovering, no matter how fit she thinks she is.'

Fiona turned to her daughter. 'Did you notice if there was something that made her change moods?'

Ashley shook her head whilst putting the cookies onto a cooling rack. 'Not really. We were in Dolly's, picking up some hamper bits, and she was laughing and getting to know Dolly again, then Ewan came in and... Wait. I went into Dolly's work studio, and when I came out, he was gone and Grace wasn't looking too good. I did ask if she was feeling all right, and she said her stomach was a bit queasy and that was all. I offered to take her home, but she wanted us to finish our day as planned. She was quiet from then on, but I just put it down to her tummy pains. Time of the month, I thought.'

Fiona glowered into her drink. 'Ewan's enough to give anyone time-of-the-month pains.'

Charlie was feeling something quite different from pain. His blood was already at boiling point, and his clenched fists were so tight, he was creating fingernail marks in his palms.

But he didn't care. The only thing on his mind was finding Ewan and punching him square in the jaw.

'What did Ewan say to her?' he asked Ashley, trying hard not to spit the words at her.

She shrugged, looking extremely sorry about leaving them alone together. 'I don't know. I wasn't listening in on their conversation. I heard something about photography, then I went out back with Dolly. I assumed they were talking shop. Do you think he said something to upset her?'

Fiona scoffed. 'It wouldn't surprise me.'

Ashley looked mortified. 'I didn't think, Mum. I would have never left her alone with him had I known he was up to something. But to be fair, we can't be entirely sure he said something to upset her. She might have just been going through the motions all by herself.'

Charlie wasn't buying that. 'Seems a bit strange she only went downhill after he showed up.'

Fiona gestured towards the kitchen doorway. 'Go and ask her, Ashley.'

Ashley shook her head whilst slapping her fish slice down. 'I'm not asking her. If she wanted to talk about it, she would have by now. She's a big girl, Mum. She needs to figure things out for herself, not have us lot keep bombarding her with questions all the time. And I'm not going to be the one who adds to her headache. It's my fault she's lost her memory.'

'Stop blaming yourself,' said Charlie softly. 'You cannot hold yourself responsible for what Viktor Blake did. The man is pure evil. He wanted to hurt you any way he could because he was jealous of you and Harrison. You have to let it go now, Ash. He's where he belongs, behind bars until his case goes to court, then he'll be put back behind bars, you can count on that. Don't let him ruin anything more for you.

Grace doesn't blame you. She told me one night. Nobody blames you.'

Fiona huffed and waggled her glass over at Charlie. 'He's right, love. It wasn't your fault. I'm just glad Grace is seeing a doctor tomorrow. Maybe she'll talk. Get some crap off her chest. Meanwhile, if I see that Ewan, I'll get *him* to talk.'

Ashley scoffed. 'Yeah, good luck with that. He wouldn't know the truth if it jumped up and bit him in the face.'

Their back and forth hate towards Ewan was becoming muffled to Charlie as the moments passed. He couldn't shake off the feeling that Ewan was the catalyst in Grace's mood change. She had been distant from him all evening, not even staying in the same room as him for more than thirty seconds. He knew her family were taking up all the space, but still, if she wanted to stand at his side, she could. The vibe was off. Grace's snub was blatant to him.

Grace entered the kitchen, stopped as though accessing the situation, appeared to know they had been talking about her, smiled weakly at Charlie, and left.

Right, that's enough of that. She's going to speak to me, whether she likes it or not.

He followed her outside into the hallway, where he was practically pinned in place by Harriet and Kerri, who wanted to talk all things Christmas with him at that very moment. He politely joined in their conversation whilst keeping one eye on the direction Grace had gone. Lopsided reindeers on rooftops and lukewarm hot chocolate drinks being served down by the beach weren't exactly drawing him in, but he tried to smile and nod where appropriate until he found his moment to escape, which was when Harrison came over and the women started to repeat themselves to him about some recent Christmas disasters.

Grace was hiding out in the empty room of the extension, quietly looking out at all the Christmas lights in the garden.

'Hey, you,' said Charlie softly, closing the door to the noise behind him.

She turned to offer a polite smile before looking back outside at the multicoloured twinkles.

Charlie approached to stand just to her side and gave her arm a playful nudge with his own. 'You okay, Grace?'

'Yeah, I'm fine.'

He glanced her way for a second, knowing she was giving him the cold shoulder. He needed her to talk to him, but it didn't look as though it were on the cards.

I just wish you would let me in. Whatever he said to you, don't believe him. You know what's he's like. Use your intuition.

Grace lifted her head a touch and turned slightly. 'I'm going to get a drink.'

He watched quietly as she walked away yet again. His shoulders dropped as a heavy sigh slowly left his nose. Not wanting to return to the crowd gathered in the other part of his home, he stepped outside into the cold air to stare up at the night sky. The stars were twinkling brightly, but even their sparkly presence failed to lift his deflated mood. Grace had her first counselling session first thing in the morning, so he hoped that would help bring her closer to him, because he had reached a point where he was starting to think he would never get her back, and that thought alone shattered his heart into a thousand pieces.

19

Grace

A white hot chocolate in a large red mug had a red-and-white candy cane hooked over the side. The drink was topped with a swirl of cream, sprinkled with a crushed raspberry boiled sweet. It sat on the low table beside Grace whilst Vivien sat the other side of her inside the Gatehouse Café.

Grace inhaled the aroma of coffee as she snuggled into one of the two red plaid armchairs close to the lit fireplace.

It was late morning and the breakfast rush had just died down, leaving Vivien free to put her feet up for all of ten minutes. She slouched back in her chair with her legs stretched out fully in front, resting a cup of tea on her stomach.

'So, come on then, out with it, Grace. How did it go this morning with the therapist?'

Grace groaned quietly and reached out to take a sip of her drink. 'Mmm, this is good, Viv. Do you just melt white chocolate into the milk?'

Vivien sat up and gave her a look that told her not to change the subject.

After a short sigh and a quick roll of the eyes, Grace plonked her drink back down and turned in her chair to face her friend. 'It wasn't really my thing, Viv.'

'It's talking to someone about your problems, Grace. How is that not anyone's thing? We all like to talk about ourselves, given the chance. Mostly, people don't let you talk, I find. So, when you've got open ears on tap, take it, that's what I say.'

Grace shrugged into her cream cable jumper. 'It didn't feel right, Viv. I said I would try, and I did. It was all right, I guess. The lady was really nice, and she gave me some helpful tips, but I don't feel the need to return anytime soon, which she did say was fine. I can call her for another appointment whenever I like.'

'Well, that's something, I suppose. What tips did she give you? You never know, they might come in handy for me.' Vivien stretched her neck, creaking it to one side.

Grace followed her eyes up to the wooden beams on the ceiling. Christmas garlands looked to be the only happy thing about the old, worn wood. 'She taught me something called worry time. You heard of that?'

'Nope. Hit me.'

'Well, instead of worrying about something all the time, you pick out a time slot and only worry about your issue during that time. Kind of like when we had a timetable at school. We wouldn't be sitting there thinking about history class while we were in maths, for example. So, we place our worry time into a timetable, say four o'clock next Wednesday. I will try that one out. It does sound helpful.'

Vivien nodded her approval. 'Yeah, I might try that myself. My worry could do with its own time slot. Saves me having to keep thinking about certain things over and over again all day.'

'I know what you mean. Gives me headache when I keep going over stuff. It just whirls around and around. Sometimes I feel as though I'm living the same situation on repeat, like Groundhog Day. Drives me insane.'

'Right, that's settled then. We're both going to practise having worry time. So, just remember, every time you start to worry, tell your mind to shut up, as it's not worry time until it's scheduled worry time.'

Grace laughed into her hand. 'Scheduled worry time. What have our lives come to?'

'I know. Remember when we hadn't a care in the world?'

'Yep. We were teenagers.'

Vivien laughed through her nose. 'That seems like yesterday sometimes. Other times, not so much. Can you believe we're in our thirties now? Where does it all go, eh, chick?'

The two women sat in companionable silence for a moment, both reminiscing over their shared past until Vivien burst out laughing. She sat up straight, crossing her legs up on the chair whilst smiling over at Grace.

'Oh my days, I just had the memory of you falling down the ditch on our way back from the Isle of Wight Festival.' She clutched at her stomach as water welled in her dark eyes. 'That was hilarious. The way your legs were sticking up in the air.'

Grace couldn't help but laugh too. 'My hip was killing me the next day.'

'Yeah, well, you were too drunk to feel anything at the time.'

'And whose fault was that, I wonder?'

Vivien tapped her chest in mock offence. 'You always blame me.'

'You were the one who made that crazy cocktail we were all drinking. I still don't know what was in it.'

'Tasted nice. I remember it was red.' She shook her head and sipped her tea. 'Nope, still can't remember what was in it. Ooh, didn't it have that rum your dad gave us?'

'Might have done. Oh, what a night that was. Can you imagine us doing anything like that these days?'

'Hey, we could still pull off a weekender. We're not that old, chick. Saying that, I think I'd need a bit more comfort these days. I'm not sure my back is up to crashing in a field all night, tent or no tent.'

Grace frowned with amusement. 'I wonder what happened to our tent. We never did find out. Do you remember that man with the long white beard who said he was going to eat all our clothes and gave us ice poles? I wonder what happened to him.'

'Oh yeah. Ice-pole Man. Oh, and what about that spotty lad you snogged.' Vivien started laughing again. 'Oh, that was just brilliant. Who on earth was he?'

'Hey, I was a teenager. We were all sharing the same vibe.'

Vivien nodded as she grinned. 'Oh, Grace, you were so funny when we were younger.' Her smile faded as she silently sighed. 'You changed so much when you started dating Ewan. Fun, bubbly Grace just disappeared.' She leaned over to pat Grace's hand. 'I hated you going out with him. You never smiled much when he was around.'

Ewan did change me. I lost my voice around him. I lost a lot of myself.

She didn't need anyone to tell her what life was like for her with him. She remembered it all. Every single word he ever said to her. All the times he blamed her, said things were broken because of her, told her she had to be the one to change. And all the time he was taking the air out of her lungs, there he was, off doing his own thing, sleeping around, not giving a stuff about her.

What did I do? Nothing, that's what. I had become too comfortable with the dark walls he had slowly built around me. I still can't believe I actually left him in the end. And that I went with Freddy.

'What you thinking, Grace?' Vivien's soft voice jolted her from her thoughts. 'You look far away.'

'Ah, I was just thinking about Freddy Morland.'

Vivien nodded slowly. 'Yeah, that was a turn up for the books. Don't think even you two saw that one coming.'

Grace shrugged. 'I guess we were just two people hurting and experimenting with those feelings.'

'He's nice, Freddy, but it was obvious he wasn't for you.'

Grace cupped her warm drink and grinned. 'I guess not, seeing as we didn't last five minutes. Viv, you should have seen my face when I woke up in the hospital to see him and our Molly all loved-up.'

Vivien snorted out a laugh. 'I can only imagine. I just wish I was there when you found out you were married to Hot Doc.'

Grace scoffed into the swirl of cream still floating in her mug. She quickly wiped it from her nose and nodded over at her grinning friend. 'He is so hot, isn't he?' Her shoulders dropped as her smile disappeared. 'I'm not sure about him though, Viv.'

Vivien looked surprised. 'What's wrong, chick? Has he done something?'

'Erm, no. He hasn't done anything.'

'Then what are you unsure of exactly? You need to elaborate here.'

'Ewan said—'

'Oh my God!'

'What?'

Vivien pursed her lips and tightened her brow. 'Ewan said. Really, Grace? You're listening to him?' She shook her head in annoyance and leaned forward in her chair. 'Stop listening to that man. Whatever comes out of his gob is a load of old crap. You know better than that.' She sat back and flapped one hand. 'What did he say?'

'He told me there are rumours about Charlie and our Ashley.'

'Oh, you are kidding me.'

Grace lowered her head, feeling stupid saying it all out loud, but she was still so confused by Ewan's statement, she needed to talk about it just to get it off her chest and hear someone else's opinion. Someone she could trust, and there was no one better than her best friend.

Vivien flapped a hand again and then sat on it in a huff. 'Okay, what rumours? What rubbish did he put in your head this time?'

She's right. He always filled my mind with crap. I couldn't breathe half the time I was around him. Why am I listening to him now?

Grace swallowed the lump in her throat and blinked away threatening tears. 'He basically said Charlie fancies Ashley, and there might have been a point where the two of them slept together or they want to.'

Vivien swore under her breath whilst shaking her head. 'I really bloody hate that man.' She shuffled in her chair so she was leaning closer to Grace. 'Please don't tell me you believed that rubbish. You know what he's like, chick. He's jealous of you. He always has been. He's such a wreck of a human being that he hates anyone who is happy and settled. He destroys every woman he goes out with. He did it to you once before and now he's trying to do it to you again. Grace, you can't let him inside your head like that. Please believe me. Listen to me.'

'I know what's he's like, Viv, but it's so hard. I'm confused most of the time anyway. I don't know what I'm supposed to be doing, or who I'm supposed to be. I don't know which way to turn half the time, and Ewan is more familiar than Charlie. It's easy to listen to him.'

Vivien tapped Grace gently on the knee, gaining eye contact. 'Okay, let's break this down a bit. Since you woke up from the coma, has anything happened that has made you smile from the inside? Anything at all?'

Grace smiled as her immediate thoughts went straight to the time Charlie took her to the Donkey Sanctuary.

Vivien joined her in smiling. 'What came to mind there, chick?'

'Charlie and the donkeys.' She watched her friend nodding her way. 'Things feel normal when it's something to do with the donkeys. When I started collecting bits for the charity hampers, I felt like my old self again.'

'But you just mentioned Charlie too.'

Grace nodded, mostly to herself at the realisation. 'He does make me smile. He gives me butterflies when I look at him.' She pulled in her lips for a moment and sighed. 'But I don't remember him.'

'I can tell you what you've told me about him in the past.'

Grace's eyes widened with curiosity and her smile returned to beam Vivien's way. 'Go on then.'

'Well, you've only ever said good things about him. You tell me you're happy. I know you're stupid-in-love with each other, as it's that obvious, and seeing how I'm your bezzie mate, I would know if something wasn't quite right between you. But, Grace, honestly, you have never been happier. You love him to pieces, and trust me when I tell you, that man has never given me any doubt to distrust him. I know we don't know what goes on behind closed doors, and that people can fool you, blah, blah, blah, but I go by you. And you came back to the land of the living when you met him. That's why I like him. Because he treats you good. And that's all anyone wants for their friend.'

Grace smiled as she placed one hand over her heart. 'Oh, Viv, you make him sound dreamy.'

'Yeah, well, I don't know about that. All I know is you have always told me he's perfect and you always felt blessed to have him in your life. But, hey, what does your gut tell you about him?'

'I think my gut likes him very much, but Ewan—'

'Oh, Ewan shpoowan. Ignore him. You had your time in the swamp, then you got yourself out. You saved you, chick. And then you straightened your shoulders, held your head high, flicked that swamp goo from your locks, and went out there into the big old wide world, and guess what? You struck gold.'

Grace lowered her head and giggled. 'You think Charlie is gold?'

'I think that's what you think of him, and I think he thinks you're pretty special too. Hey, chick, you married this one. Do yourself a favour and give him a chance. And for the love of all that is holy, stay away from Ewan.'

'So you don't think anything is going on between Charlie and Ashley?'

'Never in a million years, Grace. But what do you see when you look at your sister?'

'I see her eyes filled with love for Harrison.'

'And what do you see in Charlie's eyes?'

Grace smiled to herself as Charlie's face swept into sight. His warm smile and soothing eyes, and his soft voice and tender touch hit her all at once, causing a flutter in her stomach and a cosiness to fill her heart. 'I see his love for me.' She looked directly at Vivien. 'I also see his pain.'

Vivien's smile was filled with sympathy. 'Yeah, this is a lot for him too.'

'I know,' Grace whispered.

'Give it more time, chick. I truly believe you two will find a way back to each other. You always say you are soulmates. If that's true, nothing can tear you apart.'

'Blimey, Viv, you should be a therapist. I could do my sessions with you.'

Vivien smiled as she flopped back in her chair. 'Hey, that's what friends are for.'

20

Charlie

Castle on the Mead was lit up ready for its guests for the evening, and Charlie was delighted to see Grace smiling from ear to ear all the way along the driveway.

'Ooh, Charlie, look at the Victorian streetlamps, they're so elegant, and I love the dressed wreaths on them. How pretty is that. Ashley's done a fantastic job here. Ooh, look at the Christmas tree. Wow, those baubles are huge. Oh, I love the Nutcrackers. We have to get a picture with one of those.'

Charlie parked the car and offered Grace his arm straight away. She snuggled into his side as they walked around the pathway that led to the grounds of the small castle.

The first thing they noticed was the dark and light stripes of a beautiful green lawn, then tall, neatly trimmed hedges twinkling with multicoloured fairy lights. Gravel pathways weaved in and out of the hedgerows, alight with colour-changing lights posing as rocks. Large flowerbeds curved here and there, and square stepping stones led to a small fountain spraying colourful-lit water from the tip of a wand belonging to an ornamental fairy.

A few people were walking around drinking hot chocolate whilst enjoying the magic of the castle's winter garden.

Charlie couldn't see Ashley or Harrison, so he led Grace straight to the fountain so they could toss in a coin and make a wish.

'Are we gonna tell each other what we wished for?' He added a cheeky wink, and Grace smiled down into her cream scarf.

'I think we both know what we wished for.'

Charlie breathed out a puff of cold air as he laughed. 'Yeah, I guess that's true.'

A gentle jingling of bells chimed along to piano music playing softly from hidden speakers. Charlie took Grace's hand and turned her in a circle before holding her close to his chest for a slow dance.

Grace giggled into his shoulder and slapped his back playfully, bringing him to a halt. They stayed perfectly still, staring into each other's eyes for what seemed like a lifetime, and Charlie was completely captivated until muffled chatter of nearby visitors woke him from his trance.

'Come on.' He tugged at Grace's arm, pulling her towards a section of garden filled with gigantic shimmering flowers and glowing fairies.

'Oh, it's so magical here, Charlie.'

He followed her eyes as she took in their surroundings with glee, and it filled every part of him just knowing she was happy.

Smile, honey. Smile and remember this moment, if nothing else.

Grace met his eyes and a hint of pink hit her cheeks. He sniffed back the cold air and tugged his brown woolly hat lower over his ears to keep out the chill, grinning to himself as Grace mimicked his actions without realising. She turned away to look down at some shining insect ornaments in amongst the verge, and he quickly snapped a photo with his phone, because if he ever lost his memory, he wanted a picture of a time when the most beautiful woman in the world was smiling to herself out of pure joy. That was definitely something he would want to see.

Grace pointed at a wood-burned sign. 'Come on, Charlie. The lake's this way.' He went to speak, but she excitedly pulled him the way the sign was directing.

The large lake had a wooden bridge arched over its dark water that housed white shimmering lily pads. Multicoloured fairy lights were twirled around each rail on the bridge, creating a sparkling glow on the tip of the water beneath, where Charlie and Grace stood.

He moved his hand slowly until his fingertips reached Grace's hand, encasing each gloved finger into his palm. The water was calm and peaceful, and Grace looked to be feeling the same way.

'I can't see any fish. Can you, Charlie?'

He pulled her back slightly from peering over the side. 'No, they're probably resting on the bottom. Unless they're hiding away from all these lights.' A popping-bubble sound appeared below them followed by a ripple. 'Ooh, there's one.'

Grace leaned into his arm as he placed his hand in his coat pocket, taking hers along with him. 'It's lovely here, isn't it? My grandad used to bring me up here when I was a kid.' She pointed behind her. 'There's a large green area over there where we would have a picnic and a game of football.'

Charlie swallowed hard as he met her face. 'Has anyone told you about your grandfather yet?'

She smiled softly as she moved her chin lower into her scarf. 'Yes, my mum told me he died. We had a moment in the hospital.' She stared at the water. 'It feels nice being here again. I believe he's watching over me.'

'I believe that too, Grace.'

'And thank you for also watching over me.'

Charlie hummed a response and rested his head upon hers. He closed his eyes for a moment, relaxing into their connection.

Grace breathed out a quiet laugh. 'I was about to say I'm glad it's just us here, but here comes some more people.'

He opened his eyes to see a family of four heading their way. Two young children excitedly jogging over to see if they could spot any magical fish, he guessed. One glance at their happiness made his heart ache for the life he was about to have with his wife before tragedy struck.

Don't think that way. I'm still blessed. Grace is alive, and that's all I need. Don't give up, Wallis. Come on, man, you've got this.

'Hey, Grace, I've got a little surprise for you tonight. Come with me.'

A red-and-gold carriage pulled by a dapple-grey and a dark-brown horse sat outside the side entrance of the castle, awaiting its passengers. Grace's face lit up with delight as Charlie helped her step up into the seat. He placed a red-check blanket over their legs and told the man driving they were ready.

Grace took a picture of the driver, who was dressed in the finest red-and-gold uniform. She then snuggled her hand in Charlie's beneath the blanket as the horses started their lap of the castle's grounds.

The couple jolted back slightly as the large white wheels rolled across the gravel, heading towards a wide footpath lined with arched framework lit up with multicoloured bulbs.

Charlie smiled at Grace's beam as they entered the tunnel of light. She moved closer to him until they could be no closer, and he felt her lightly squeeze his arm. The clip-clop of hooves, the odd snuffle from the horses, and the turning of the wheels along the path were the only sounds he could hear, and that somehow relaxed his weary soul. Her head came closer to his, so he dipped to rest his upon her red woolly hat.

Grace fidgeted and shuffled, turning her face his way, causing him to meet her halfway. There was a glassy look in her blue eyes and the slightest of smiles upon her cold lips, and Charlie couldn't hold his love inside. He leaned over and met her mouth with his own. The coldness of their noses warmed against their skin, and he placed one gloved hand upon her cheek to help keep out the chill, and because he wanted to touch her so badly.

'I love you, Grace,' he whispered into their kiss.

She cupped his face, pulling him closer towards her. She heated the moment, taking him further into her mouth whilst positioning one of her legs over his lap. Charlie immediately reached for her hip to help lift her all the way onto him, as all thoughts of where they were slipped his mind. Grace's lips trailed down his neck, and he was lost in her. She tugged at his scarf, giving herself more access to his body, and he happily helped by pulling it free. The cold air gripped his throat and a bump along the pathway woke him out of his trance.

'Grace.' He lifted her forward so he could see her face. She looked flushed and in need of everything he wanted to give her.

She leaned closer, resting her forehead on his. 'Take me home, Charlie. Take me to bed.'

Under normal circumstances, he wouldn't have to be told twice. But he still had the wariness in him of her waking the next day filled with regrets. He placed her back on the seat and tenderly kissed her cheek.

'Okay, Grace,' he whispered, as his voice had vanished along with his willpower.

She stroked over the side of his face, not taking her eyes off him, which only filled him with way more butterflies than he knew he possessed. In that moment he loved her more than ever.

They both gasped quietly as soft snowflakes began to fall, and Grace reached out a hand to watch them fade into her glove.

'Oh, Charlie, could tonight be any more magical?'

Charlie couldn't help but smile. He gave her a cheeky wink as she turned back his way. 'Oh, I do hope so, Grace.'

21

Grace

The snow was falling thick and fast outside Waterside Cottage, creating a crisp white blanket over everything and bringing a blue hue to the cold night. Inside, central heating warmed the home, and a crackling fire in the living room emitted a soft glow over Grace's naked body as she slowly lowered herself backwards over the rug in front of the fireplace, arching her back as Charlie's lips traced across her stomach.

Every touch he made felt familiar and welcomed, and she quickly discovered she had no shame in front of him. She relaxed, enjoying how he held her, how he made her feel, and how he warmed her heart.

Charlie mumbled out Grace's name over and over as he made his way all around her body, leaving no part untouched or unloved, and Grace could do little but fall deeper into the new feeling the connection was bringing.

Their mouths met, and Grace was sure she would tumble over the edge at any moment. She raked her fingers through his hair, gripped him, and pulled him closer. She had a moment where she wondered if they used condoms, or if they were trying for a baby again before the accident. A hundred thoughts flashed through her mind, each one kissed away by the man she married.

Charlie's hands reached down to lift her bottom, and Grace lost all interest in thinking about anything that didn't involve his naked body pressed against hers.

She gripped his back and sank her mouth into his neck as his lips trailed her collarbone. His muffled sounds illuminated her more than any Christmas lights she'd seen that night. She could listen to him forever, and really wanted to. She wrapped her legs around him, holding him in place as she decided to whisper something back to him.

'Charlie, I want you.'

He stilled for a second, then made them as close as they could possibly be, and Grace experienced a feeling deep within her soul that outweighed the rush attempting to take over her body. No amount of stars in the sky or butterflies in her belly could show her what magic really was. Charlie Wallis had cornered the market, and Grace had been well and truly swept off her feet.

There was no come down as Charlie rested by her side. Grace was still in the clouds, soaring amongst the most incredible sunset she had ever seen. Rainbows sparkled before her eyes as fairy dust rained down upon her hair. She took a slow and steady breath, but still the huge smile covering her face would not leave. Her heart was full with the rays from the sun, and her body had been warmed by the touch of pure love. She had no words, just a feeling. A strong, powerful feeling that refused to disappear, which pleased her, as she didn't want to live another day without it wrapped around her very existence.

Grace moved her head sideways to look at his beautiful face. His eyes were closed and the hint of a smile warmed his peaceful expression.

There was something so serene about the moment, not to mention surreal. She wasn't quite sure what to do next, as lying there beside him whilst feeling so carefree and happy made it feel as though nothing else mattered. She turned to stare up at the ceiling and had another déjà vu moment.

Ignoring it completely, she sat up and twisted her legs so she was turned towards Charlie.

One eye opened and then the other, and his slight smile broadened. 'How you doing up there?'

The huskiness in his voice brought her lips straight down onto his, and he reacted by cupping her face, then around her head, wrapping her hair over both their faces. Their kiss deepened quickly, and Charlie flipped her over, pinning her back to the rug, but Grace was in no mood to be in the passenger's seat. She scrambled out from beneath him and rolled onto her knees, then gently peppered his whole body with kisses after placing his hands behind his head. Her silent way of telling him to relax.

There was so much about Charlie that simply felt right, and she wanted to show him she was going to give their relationship her best shot, because even if she never remembered the man he was, she was determined to get to know the man she had right now. The man smiling up at her with so much love in his eyes. The man she was happy to keep kissing until the sun came up.

'I love kissing you, Charlie.'

He gripped her hips as she straddled his lap. 'That's funny, I feel the same way.'

She lowered herself so she was nose to nose with him. 'You make my heart smile.'

He held back her hair and pulled her lips to his own. 'I don't have enough words to tell you how much I love you.'

'I don't have any words. Just a whole bunch of feelings.' She smiled and kissed his nose. 'Feelings for you.'

'Are they new or old?'

She gave a tiny shrug and met his mouth again. 'I don't know. I just know there are a lot of them.'

'Thank you for giving me a chance, Grace,' he mumbled on her lips.

'Thank you for not giving up on me, Charlie.'

He held her face so he was looking directly in her eyes. 'I'd never give up on you, honey. You give me life.'

'Charlie, you say the loveliest things to me.'

'I love you, Grace, and I know you can't make any promises to me, but I'm asking you now, please, don't ever leave me.'

Grace sat up, a tad startled by his plea. He sounded desperate, as though he were expecting her to up and leave any moment. She placed her hand over his heart and smiled down at him. 'I don't feel like I would leave.'

'You might change your mind in the morning.'

She shook her head slightly. 'I don't feel I will.'

Charlie sat up with her still on his lap. One of his hands held her back in place whilst the other rested by his side on the rug. 'I hope you stay feeling this way about me.'

Grace dipped her head to settle upon his. 'Charlie,' she whispered. 'I want to be your wife. In every sense.'

It was the smallest of sounds, but she heard the whoosh of strangled air leave his lungs. She gently raised his head to see a lone teardrop roll down his cheek. Slowly, she swiped her fingertip beneath his eye, then pressed her lips lightly upon his closed eyelid.

'Don't cry, Charlie. I've got you,' she whispered.

He drew her closer as his deep sigh filled the silence. 'I've got you too, Grace.'

She lifted his chin higher so she could see his glassy eyes. 'That's all right then. If we've got each other, we'll be okay.'

He nodded into her palm and smiled weakly, and Grace pulled him back into her chest where she hugged him as tightly as he was hugging her, only letting go when they had to loosen their grip to help with breathing. She glanced at the fire, mesmerised by its flames for a moment. A waft of Christmas tree floated her way followed by the sound of a gust of wind from outside.

She stroked over his shoulder as she looked at the closed drapes covering the back door. 'I'm glad we're inside.'

'Yeah, we're lucky in many ways.' His voice was so quiet and broken, she gave him another hug.

The gentle sweep of his fingertips over her bare back brought on a shiver of delight. His mouth on her neck added to the feeling, causing her to push herself further into him.

'Charlie,' she whispered close to his ear before nibbling on his lobe. 'I want to make love all night. You up for that?'

Within two seconds flat, he showed her exactly how up for that quest he was, and Grace was right back in her magical world of moonbeams and stardust, which she made sure she visited as many times as she could before sleep deprivation took control and consumed them both.

22

Charlie

The snow had made everything bright outside, and Charlie was so glad he was snuggled in his warm bed with Grace by his side. The breakfast tray he had brought her sat at their feet, and a large beige photo album was on his lap.

'You gave me this on our first anniversary.' He slid the book over to her. 'I think maybe now is a good time for you to take a peek.'

Grace stroked the cover and then slowly flipped the page. She frowned up at him when her eyes met the picture of two disposable cups sitting on a wall. 'Did I take this?'

Charlie nodded as he grinned. He snuggled further into her and kissed her cheek. 'This album shows our first year together. All these photos tell the story of us falling in love.'

Grace tapped the picture. 'What story does that tell?'

'Okay, here's what happened. We met in the Santa booth, right?' He watched her nod. 'I thought I'd buy you a hot chocolate when we came out, but by the time I came back, you had walked away with your sisters. So, with heavy heart, I put them down and left.' She went to speak, but he raised one finger. 'However, unbeknown to me, you saw me lower my head in defeat, place the drinks down, and walk away. You ran over, but I was already lost in the crowd, and that's when you snapped the shot.'

'That's the story?'

'Yep, that's the story. Strange, I know.'

Grace laughed and turned the page whilst mumbling about the two white cups.

Next was a headshot of Charlie, flashing just a trace of a smile straight into the camera.

'Your work photo?'

He placed one arm around her shoulders, pulling her closer, and smooshed his face into her hair. 'That's the second time we met.' He breathed out a quiet laugh and shook his head. 'You have no idea how happy I was that day. I didn't have long so rushed in, expecting to stay all of two minutes, and there you were. All set up, looking professional and somewhat startled at first, but then your face softened, your smile widened, and you came over to show me where to sit, even though it was obvious, as the one and only chair was right in front of the tripod.'

Grace laughed and nudged his side. 'Hey, I was probably just being polite.'

'Nah, you wanted me, that's why you moved in on my personal space.'

'I bet you didn't mind.'

'Oh, honey, you have no idea.'

Grace pointed to the next picture. 'And what's this one all about?'

The wooden salt and pepper pots holding up a pizza menu on a red-check dressed table next to a bottle of red wine looked Insta-worthy, giving off cosy vibes of a good night.

'Our first date. Do you recognise the place?'

She slowly bobbed her head as she homed in on the photo. 'Yeah, it's Mama's Love.' She turned to face him. 'That was our first date?'

'Part of it. We ate there first, then headed over to the cinema, as they were showing Christmas movies all month.' He gestured towards a selfie of them both in their seats, with popcorn on their laps and smiles upon their faces. 'Our first selfie, taken just before the movie started.'

'Oh, I can see we're in the back row. Did any snogging take place?'

Charlie gave her shoulder a gentle squeeze. 'Hey, it was our first date. I was a gentleman, I'll have you know. I waited for the appropriate moment for that kiss.'

Grace crinkled her nose as she frowned. 'What's the appropriate moment?'

'You know. When you walk a girl to her door.'

'And that's where we kissed?'

'Firstly, I would just like to explain I was only going in for a kiss on the cheek, but I stayed way too long pressed there, and you didn't go anywhere, so I slowly moved around your face until our lips met.' He re-enacted the moment, making her giggle on his mouth. 'I couldn't help myself.'

'Did it get heated?'

'No. It was a slow, steady, tender kiss that held all the emotions of a thousand love stories.'

'Aww, Charlie. That's really sweet.'

'You're sweeter.'

She snuggled further into the duvet and smiled. 'And is that when you fell in love with me?'

Charlie leaned down with her and nudged her nose with his own. 'No. I fell in love with you in the Santa booth.'

'And there was me thinking you were a man of science. Do you really believe in love at first sight?'

'I can't exactly argue with it when it happened to me.' He shrugged and turned back to the photo album.

'So, when did I know I loved you? Have I ever told you?'

'Yeah, I know the story. It took you a bit longer than me, which was okay. In my mind, I had already married you. You just had to catch up.'

Grace stroked the side of his face. 'How long did I take?'

'Ah, not long. You fell in love with me straight away, you were just so wary of men, it took you a while to admit your feelings to yourself. You tried holding back, but I hung on in there, and you finally realised I was a good guy.'

'You are a good guy. I think.'

'Hmm. Well, anyway, I think that was why you documented our journey. You didn't just take pictures, you started your diary, and you had your good and bad jars.'

'My what?'

Charlie glanced over at the wardrobe. 'They're in there somewhere. Two chunky jars that once held what you would call coffee. Yucky granules. You would write mini statements on a piece of paper, fold it, number it, then pop it into the relevant jar. One day, you decided to open them up to see what you had. I think you were trying to weigh me up. Anyway, you had loads of good notes, and no bad. None at all. You found me and declared your undying love right there and then.'

'Oh, wow. What do I sound like? How did that make you feel? It can't be good, figuring out your relationship that way.'

'Hey, Grace, it's okay. You were still healing from your past. I understood. We took each day as it came. And, as it happened, each day was just as good as the last. We worked. We were fine. And you started to relax.'

She hovered her hand over their first selfie. 'How was I that night?'

'We had a laugh. We always laughed.' Her warm smile was melting his heart.

'What Christmas film did we see?'

'The choice was between *Die Hard* and *Gremlins*.' He shuffled around so he could watch her try to figure out which movie they picked.

'Technically, neither of those are Christmas films.'

Yes, we had that conversation at the time. Let's see what you say this time.

'Oh, why is that?'

'Well, in order for it to be a Christmas film, it has to be about Christmas, not just set at Christmas. Both those films are set at that time of year, that's all. Although don't tell Ashley I said that. She's a *Die Hard* fan, and she says that it is very much a Christmas film.'

Wow, those were the exact words she said back then.

'Anyway,' she added. 'I'm going to choose *Gremlins* as the film we watched.'

'Spot on.'

Grace smiled, looking very pleased with herself.

'Check this out.' Charlie turned the page to reveal a photograph of him paddling in the sea at Sandly Beach. 'Our first beach day together. In January. Yep. New Year's Day. Totally your idea, and, yes, I did freeze. But it sure was fun getting warm afterwards.'

'Oh my goodness, and where exactly did we warm up?'

'Right here, honey. Your favourite place in the world.'

Grace raised her brow in amusement. 'My favourite place in the world is your bed?'

'Our bed, and no. Waterside Cottage is what I meant.' He watched her stroke the bed covers as though just realising it was her bed. 'We had hot chocolate with marshmallows in front of the fire, curled in a patchwork blanket. Butt naked.'

'I do like marshmallows.'

'Really? That's all you're gonna take from that moment?'

Grace muffled her giggle by squishing his knuckles onto her lips. 'Marshmallows are important, Charlie.'

'Okay, well, you've got me there. Marshmallows are good this time of year.'

'Like strawberries in June.'

He closed the album and lowered it to the floor so he could snuggle down in bed with Grace in his arms. 'Yeah, just like strawberries in June.' He tenderly kissed her mouth and grinned as he felt her smile on his lips. 'What are you so happy about, huh?'

'Marshmallows,' she whispered, teasing him with her eyes.

'I know something way more magical than marshmallows in the winter.' He lowered his mouth to her neck and peppered kisses down to her collarbone.

Grace moaned quietly and moved finding his mouth with her own. Her fingers were in his hair and one of her legs was curled around his knee. 'What's that?'

Charlie pulled back, grinning down at her. 'Snow days.'

Her eyebrows lifted along with her mouth. 'Snow days?'

He gestured to the window and nodded. 'Today, Grace Wallis, we're gonna have ourselves a snow day.'

She shuffled up onto her elbows and peered over at the window. 'How much is out there?'

'Enough. So come on. Get up. An unassembled snowman awaits us.' He climbed out of bed and headed for the bathroom, pleased with his day so far. A hot shower, some warm clothes, a hearty breakfast, and then snow, snow, snow. He had a plan, and it seemed as though it were going to be another productive day, especially the part when they came in from the cold and enjoyed another hot shower that would be swiftly followed by a snuggle on the sofa whilst watching *Gremlins*, and, of course, eating marshmallows.

The hot water poured over Charlie, soothing his aching lower back and the damage to his heart that Grace's accident had caused. A quick prayer in the shower every morning was pretty much routine. Every day he asked for Grace to find her memories, and each day he believed something was working, because she often seemed so close to him. He found it a lot easier to pray than to sink his head into a bottle of whisky. Faith was important to him, and Grace even more. He could never stop believing she would return, or at the very least, she would fall in love with him all over again.

Charlie flicked through some of his own memories from their first year together. The surfing. The hot air balloon trip. Their first picnic. The cherries they playfully threw at each other during a walk through Hope Park. The wishes they made at Wishing Point, and the night they kissed in their garden under a thousand twinkling stars, feeling as though they would never be able to stop. Dancing on the beach at the Mermaid Festival was magical and funny. She took his breath away a million times over during her interpretive dance to 'Tiny Dancer'.

He closed his eyes, about to quietly sing the song to take himself back to that moment. The golden sand beneath his bare feet, the salty taste in his mouth wafting in the gentle sea breeze, and the love of his life twisting and turning to the beat. He sang to her that day, and she joined in, making everything perfect. She was singing now, merging with his thoughts somehow. He opened his eyes as Grace entered the shower and leaned close to his back.

The noise of the water did little to hide her voice as she sang the song along his shoulders. He turned, and she continued to sing 'Tiny Dancer' upon his cheek and then his neck. Grace smiled, grabbed his hand, and spun in a circle. She placed her arms in the air and swayed, allowing his voice to join in and carry over hers and the noise of the shower.

Charlie placed his hands on her hips and lowered his head so it rested on her chin, swaying with her as the music filled them.

The slightest of movements, the change in tempo, the sound of the falling water mixed with her soft voice in his ear took his breath away once more. He raised his eyes to meet sea-blue ones sparkling with pure joy. Every fibre of his being was lost in her, knowing she had no idea how much that song meant to them.

Feel our song. Take it into your heart and own it. It's yours, honey. The first time we danced on golden sand to each and every note.

Grace curled her arms around Charlie's shoulders and pulled him closer for a slow dance, and just like that, she was making a new memory for them. He was the only one who knew they had never danced in the shower before. She needed to know. Without a photograph or a note in a jar, this was something she could wrap her mind around and hold on to.

'Grace, this is our first shower dance you're creating.'

She rested her head upon his shoulder and snuggled closer, smooshing her face into his neck and warming his body with her own. 'And I'll never forget it. Never in a million years.'

'Neither will I, honey.'

'This could be our song.' She raised her head slightly to gaze up at him. 'Or do we already have one?'

'We have this one, Gracie. This is our song.'

'Because I just made it so?'

He gently kissed her lips, then sighed deeply into her damp hair. 'No, honey, because you made it so one night when we danced on Sandly Beach.'

She gasped and raised her head to face him. 'I saw you in the shower, and this song popped into my head, and I just felt the need to dance with you. Oh, Charlie, what does it mean?'

'It means that even though your mind isn't working too well at the moment, your heart is doing just fine.'

23

Grace

Grace tapped the bell on her Christmas jumper and laughed to herself as it jingled. She glanced over the kitchen at Charlie and laughed at his jumper as well. At least hers was all trees and sparkles. His was some sort of psychedelic snowman on a surfboard. She had no idea where he purchased that from, but it hadn't failed to make her smile all morning, along with the fact that somehow she had managed to remember their song, even though she didn't know it was their song. Still, she was holding on to it with both hands, certain it was a good sign.

Charlie closed the fridge door and held a carrot aloft. 'I have a nose.' His face was filled with childlike glee, warming her heart even more than their shared shower.

'There are quite a few scarves in the cloakroom. We can use one of those. Erm, why do we have so many? Was I a scarf addict or something, or is that you?'

Charlie laughed as he rummaged around in the cupboard. 'No, that would be Molly.' He glanced over his shoulder and rattled a jar filled with currants. 'I think these might be too small for eyes. Molly went through a knitting faze a while back. Harrison knits now. He's already made two scarves. What should we use for eyes?'

'Stones. We'll dig some out in the back garden. So, Molly was knitting, eh? They're actually really good. I'm sure she won't mind if we use one of her creations. I'll wash it afterwards.' Grace peered out the window and couldn't help but smile. 'I love snow.'

'Yep, I know you do.'

Outside was cool and fresh, and the deep snow was crunchy and made everything look clean and bright. With their wellies on and coats buttoned, Grace and Charlie built the biggest snowman they could muster. A few snowballs were tossed back and forward in between, and laughter mingled in with the air.

Grace stepped back to admire their handiwork. 'Why does our snowman look familiar?'

Charlie gave it the once over. 'I think they all kind of look that way, honey.'

'Ooh, I think it's the scarf. Isn't that the same colour as the one we used in Lapland?'

'Oh, you checked out the honeymoon pictures. I was gonna show you the album you created, but I wasn't entirely sure where it was. I thought it was with the wedding album, but nope. Where did you find it?'

Grace frowned with confusion as she slowly stomped her way through the snow, circling the snowman. 'I didn't. I just knew the scarf was red.' She met his wide eyes as she raised one soaked gloved hand to her mouth. 'Charlie, am I right?'

His smile appeared, and he bent to scoop some snow to throw her way. 'Yep.'

Grace watched the white flakes disperse into the slight breeze around her. Her smile widened as much as his, causing her heart to warm her body.

I remembered something again, sort of. Oh, flipping heck, will this ever come back to me? It's so frustrating.

A snowball smacked her in the shoulder, jolting her straight out of the tension headache about to make an appearance.

Charlie laughed, then flopped to the ground to make snow angels. Flapping his arms and legs, he called for Grace to join him, which she did with little thought.

'Did we do this in Lapland?' she asked, mid-laugh.

'Of course. More than once.' He stopped to settle inside his snow angel, then lifted to rest upon one elbow, facing her way. 'Hey, Grace, you ever kissed inside a snow angel?'

She giggled and peered his way. 'Your angel or mine?' Before she could inhale, he was resting over her, with his damp nose pressing on hers. She laughed and reached up to wipe both their noses before they dripped. 'So, this is new as well, is it?'

'Yeah. Now I'm wondering why we didn't make out inside our snow angels in Lapland.'

Grace pulled him to her mouth, creating some warmth. 'I'm glad we're doing it now,' she whispered as they came up for air.

'Me too.' He gave her a peck on the cheek, then pulled himself up, taking her along with him. 'I think our Christmas jumper day also needs to be a trip to see the reindeers day.' He glanced over at the house. 'The roads shouldn't be too bad. The snow isn't that deep. I think old Sunflower can make it.' He took her hand, walking back to their door. 'I'll send a message to the Pepper Bay group chat. See if anyone knows if the main roads are drivable.'

Grace pulled off her outerwear as soon as she stepped back inside the cosy cottage, feeling blessed for her home.

It will be hard if I don't get my memory back fully, but it won't be so bad, not now I know what my future looks like.

That was it. She had made up her mind. She was staying with Charlie, quitting professional photography and Tuesday Club, and was going to ask her husband how he felt about trying again for a baby the following year.

Yes, that sounds like a plan. That's the life I want. Charlie's who I want. Whatever happens from this moment on, at least I have him.

Grace quickly swiped away a tear and sniffed, swallowing down her overwhelming emotions. She looked around the hallway for Charlie, but he was still in the kitchen, no doubt seeing if they could visit the zoo.

Ewan came to mind. His voice. His words. How convincing and perfectly normal he seemed. Her past with him suddenly flashed through her, as though watching her life play out like a film. All the badness and sadness appeared, and she remembered him for who he truly was. She mentally shook her head at herself, unable to believe he had reeled her in once more.

She knew the man better than anyone, and although she didn't know Charlie as well just yet, the one thing she could say was, Charlie Wallis made her feel alive, and Ewan never gave her that. He made her feel as though she were dying. Death by a thousand cuts. A slow and tortuous relationship that went nowhere fast.

Wow! He really did suck the life out of me. Right, that's it. Ewan is dead to me. If I see him again, I'm going to tell him exactly where he can go. He is never getting inside my head again.

'Grace, the zoo is closed,' Charlie called from the kitchen. He appeared in the doorway, gesturing towards the phone in his hand. 'The main roads were gritted last night, but the country lanes are covered. Tessie put out a message on the Pepper Bay group chat.'

'Charlie, I have something I want to tell you.'

He lowered his phone and raised his eyebrows. 'You in pain?'

'No, no. It's not that. It's about Ewan.' She watched his face fall flat. 'He made me think you and Ashley were close.'

'Close?'

'That you like her way more than a sister-in-law.' She could feel the tension from across the hallway. 'I got confused at first. That's why I was distant the other day. But I see him for who he is now. Plus, Vivien told me off for listening to him. I know Ashley would never do anything like that to me, and I believe you wouldn't either. I want to let you know.' She took a breath and lowered her eyes to the floor. 'I'm sorry, Charlie. He got into my head for a moment. I don't know what has happened in the last four years, so it felt as though he was just filling in some gaps for me. I didn't know what to believe.'

Charlie quickly approached her and wrapped her in his arms. 'Hey, it's okay, Grace. I know what he's like as well. He won't be coming anywhere near you ever again.'

She lifted her face to meet the anger in his eyes that softened as soon as he looked her way. 'I don't want any trouble. Promise me you won't do anything.'

'I wasn't going to. I promise. I'm just not letting him near you again if we see him. I'm not gonna lie to you, Grace. I want to punch him in the face, but you know I don't go out of my way to have a fight. Well, I guess you don't know that, but now you do. I'm not confrontational, but with him, I just want to smack him every time I see his smug face.'

'I want him out of my life for good. No trouble, no interaction, no nothing. I don't want to entertain him, but the next time I see him, I will be letting him know I don't want him to talk to me ever again. Then I'll walk away. People like him are best left ignored. He'll not get any more of my energy.'

Charlie kissed her forehead and sighed deeply. 'I can talk to him for you. You don't have to deal with that.'

'It's okay. I want to. He's a nasty piece of work, and he always attacked me when I was low, making sure I stayed down. His words are filled with an invisible venom that others don't see. You'd have to be his partner to know what he's truly like. It was hard for me back then, but also hard for me now. I know I'm vulnerable because of my head injury. I don't need people like him taking advantage.'

Charlie stepped back, holding her at arm's length. He smiled warmly as he nodded slowly. 'I'm glad you figured that out by yourself. I hoped you would. You did four years ago. You saved yourself from him back then, and now you've done it again. You, Grace Wallis, are incredible, and I'm so proud of you.'

Grace breathed out a laugh through her nose and took a bow. 'I guess I'm not as stupid as I look.'

They laughed, then hugged again.

I made changes. I took chances. I allowed my heart to fly free, and look where it took me. I can't believe how happy I am.

Grace gazed into Charlie's eyes as though he were the best thing since sliced bread, and he returned the look.

'Hey, Grace. I've got something better than the zoo we can do today. Come with me. You are gonna love this. I promise.'

She happily slipped her hand into his and followed him to their bedroom, expecting to get hot and steamy with her husband, especially when he closed the curtains, which was unnecessary, seeing as they had no close neighbours who would be able to see through their window.

'I bought this a while back, but we've never used it,' said Charlie, rummaging around in the wardrobe.

Grace frowned at the old-fashioned projector contraption that made an appearance along with Charlie's happy face.

'Ta-dah!' he announced, then proceeded to set it up at the end of the bed.

'What on earth is that thing?'

'I saw it online. It projects images onto the ceiling. Settle back, honey, and watch.'

Grace snuggled down into the plump pillows, throwing a couple on the floor, as there were far too many upon the bed. She guessed she went overboard at the bedding shop one time. She sighed happily whilst Charlie faffed about with the old machine, then giggled when he jumped on the bed and flopped to her side, excitement oozing from him.

'Check this out.' He pointed up, then clicked the one-button remote.

Grace stared up at the dullness of the white ceiling, wondering what image was going to pop up, then gasped with surprise as the Northern Lights appeared.

Charlie tapped on his phone, causing soft music to fill the room, then snuggled close to her, holding her hand. 'As soon as you want, we'll go back to see them for real, but for now, this is for you,' he whispered close to her ear.

Waterside Cottage had disappeared, as the bedroom entered another realm, and Grace was so in awe of the imagery, she forgot altogether she hadn't really been transported anywhere. The swirls of colours and relaxing music soothed her soul and removed all the damage in her head, replacing it with pure magic.

'I love you, Charlie,' she whispered. She felt him gently squeeze her hand, then kiss her cheek, and she met the warmth in his eyes as she shuffled her head on the pillow.

'Marry me. Marry me again.'

24

Charlie

'Oh my fishnet stockings, we have so much to do in such a small space of time,' said Fiona, flapping her arms to her sides whilst marching around the kitchen in Waterside Cottage. 'We've got to send out invites and get more food than our Ashley has ordered for the castle's Christmas Eve party.' She glared over at Grace, who was sitting at the table, sipping orange juice. 'People think they're going to a party. We've got raffles and sausage rolls. Are you sure you want to renew your vows that day, baby girl? I'm sure we can do better than sausage rolls.'

'What's wrong with sausage rolls all of a sudden? We had them at my wedding.' Grace paused for thought. 'I think. Did we?' she asked Charlie.

Before he had a chance to reply, Fiona clapped her hands together loudly. 'Ooh, you did. She remembers. She remembers,' she cheered. 'That's it, we're buying all the sodding sausage rolls we can find.' She slapped Grace on the back as she passed her by, causing Grace to splutter her drink. 'I need to make some calls.' Fiona darted for the front door.

Grace wiped her mouth and turned to Charlie as he sat down by her side. 'Am I really remembering sausage rolls?'

Charlie grinned and bit into a croissant. 'Guess so,' he mumbled through his food.

'What a thing to remember.'

'We can have a sausage roll tower wedding cake.' He swallowed down his mouthful and laughed, not realising Grace would take the idea seriously.

'That's what we're going to have. We'll put a little bride and groom on top. It will kill Mum but be so hilarious. I love it. It's so happening.'

Charlie wiped a flake from his mouth before leaning over to kiss her cheek. 'Whatever you want, honey. It will certainly be different, that's for sure.'

Grace shuffled in her chair to face him, placing her legs in between his. 'Will your family be able to get here for Christmas Eve? I know it's short notice.'

'Yeah. They've already booked rooms at Hotel Royale in Sandly.'

Grace smiled widely as she placed both her hands over her heart. 'Oh, Charlie, we're really doing this.'

'Yep. Then we're off to Lapland. How do you like those apples?'

'I like them very much. Just not as much as sausage rolls.' She leaned forward, kissing his lips softly.

Fiona whizzed back in the kitchen. 'We got a ton of sausage rolls. Nora called Lena, who called Roddy down at the supermarket, and he's ordered extra just for us.'

Wow! People work fast around here.

'Mum, we're not having a traditional wedding cake. We've decided to have a tower of sausage rolls with the bride and groom on top.'

'Oh, that's fantastic,' said Kerri, pushing a pram into the room.

'Why sausage rolls?' asked Harriet, following her sister. She grabbed the rest of the croissant from Charlie's plate and stuffed the non-chewed end in her mouth.

'Because our Gracie remembered having them at her wedding,' said Fiona, with a face filled with pride. She set about making tea for everyone, whether they wanted any or not.

'What a thing to remember,' said Molly, walking in. 'Mind you, doesn't every function have sausage rolls? It wouldn't be a party without them.'

Lexi joined the busy kitchen. 'Dad said he's going to make onion tartlets for the party, but Ashley's moaning.'

'I'm not moaning,' said Ashley, sliding past Harrison in the doorway.

Great, Harrison is here. Now I'm not outnumbered by Hadleys. Not that I care what food we have. My wife wants to marry me again. That's all I need.

He glanced her way as she left the chair next to him to plop her heavily pregnant sister Lexi there instead. Grace returned the gentle smile he was offering, then set about making more toast.

I better get out more fruit. Looks like the whole family are here for breakfast this morning. Even Harrison's grinning at me. Yeah, I know, this lot are on top form today.

He pulled out some tubs of washed and prepared fruit chunks, then placed them on the table, sliding the tomato sauce towards Lexi, who happily plopped a dollop onto her remaining croissant.

Harrison caught his eye, gesturing towards the hallway, so Charlie stepped outside, glad to lose the acoustics coming from the kitchen. He beckoned Harrison to the living room, only to find Ronnie sitting on the sofa next to Lexi's partner, Bryce.

Ronnie was talking all things veg, and Bryce seemed to be listening.

Harriet's partner, Jude, was talking to Freddy, leaving Charlie to wonder where Kerri's partner, Toby, was. Knowing Toby was studying to be a doctor, and remembering what that was like, he figured Toby was studying hard somewhere.

Harrison gestured towards the back door, so Charlie followed him into the garden. The air was mild, and what was left of the snow was keeping the ground looking nice and clean.

'You all right, Charlie? It's a bit manic in there.'

Charlie breathed out a laugh. 'You're the one who wanted some peace and quiet. I can tell.'

Harrison grinned. 'Hey, we're in this together.'

'Seriously though, H. Is it gonna be a bit much turning your Christmas Eve party into our wedding? I didn't know Grace was going to call Ashley as soon as I said yes to her proposal.'

'It's fine. Honest. Everything's set up anyway. All you have to do is turn up and say a few words to each other. Then we party. Your part will only take ten minutes. Then we can get on with the raffle.'

They both laughed.

Ah, man, life is getting weirder and weirder. I've got a wife who can't remember me, a sausage roll wedding cake, and for the first time ever, I'm not missing my job.

'You want to come up to the castle to see where you'd like to stage the event? We don't have an altar, but the Green Room, as Ashley calls it, has a lovely vibe. Ash was up all night, talking weddings. I've hardly had any sleep. We haven't got a licence to hold proper weddings yet. Not that yours isn't proper. Oh, you know what I mean. We just don't need a licence for you and Grace to tell each other how much you're still in love.' Harrison smiled, then added. 'Hey, how's she doing?'

'Better. She still has ups and downs, but more ups now. She's figured a lot out about her life by herself and kind of knows where she wants to be. She's not really into the photography anymore. I mean, she likes it, but not as a profession. Her heart is with those donkeys, more than anything else.'

'Aww, I love donkeys.'

'Everyone loves donkeys.'

'Now there's an idea. Perhaps you could get a few up at the castle for the big day.'

Charlie nodded, liking that idea. 'I'll have to speak to Red. Grace has a favourite donkey called Mistletoe. It would be great if we could at least get that one.'

Harrison grinned. 'Got to love a bit of brainstorming.'

Charlie had to laugh. 'Can't say I've ever talked donkeys and sausage roll cakes before.' He had another thought. 'Hey, H, how quickly do you think you could make me a ring? I'd like to give Grace a new one to represent our new start.'

'Seeing how I'm the best jeweller in the world, it shouldn't be a problem. What have you got in mind?'

'She doesn't like anything flashy. How about a platinum band? She used to say her gold one didn't match all her clothes. This way, she can swap whenever she wants.'

Charlie realised Grace hadn't put her wedding ring back on since her stay in hospital. She always took it off for work. He wondered if she ever thought about it.

You'll have a new one soon, Mrs Wallis.

'Sure. Leave it with me. That will be no problem. I haven't got much on at the moment, what with Ashley roping me in to get the castle back on the map. I still have to keep my jewellery business up and running though. We definitely need that money rolling in.' Harrison swirled one foot into the snowy edge of a planter. 'Erm, I don't mean to pry, Charlie, but are you okay for money? I can always help you out, if need be. Please don't ever feel you can't ask.'

Charlie patted Harrison on the shoulder. 'Thanks. I appreciate the offer, but we're okay. I've always been a great saver. My mother taught me from an early age how to budget, spend, and save. I had it embedded in me that it's important to always have something stashed away for a rainy day. Besides, I'm on holiday pay at the moment. Plus, my parents keep texting me, asking if I need money. I'm good, seriously, but thanks.'

Harrison nodded and gestured inside. 'Let's go get a cuppa and see what the latest is on your big day.'

'Oh, please. I dread to think what Fiona has come up with. She's more excited than anyone.'

'Onion tartlets,' called Ronnie as they stepped back into the living room.

Oh, I'm really not a fan.

'Sounds good to me, Ron.' Charlie gave him the thumbs-up, and Bryce turned to grin.

Jude patted Charlie on the back as he followed him out to the hallway. 'That's what I love about Canadians. Always polite.'

Charlie threw his arm around Jude's shoulder. 'Yeah, well, you Yanks should take note.'

'Hey, I'm from Malibu. We're all chilled there. Politeness is part of our set-up.'

Harrison frowned. 'God, I feel really boring around you two.'

'Come out to America,' said Jude, grinning. 'The women will love your English accent. Trust me.'

'Erm, he's staying put, thank you very much,' said Ashley, leaving the kitchen. She planted a kiss on Harrison's cheek and brushed back his light-brown hair with one swipe.

He lowered his head and kissed her below her ear. 'I'm not going anywhere unless you're there.'

Ashley grinned. 'Well, in that case, we're definitely up for a trip to your hometown, Jude. Perhaps next autumn.'

'October might be good for us,' said Harriet, joining them. She swung her arm around Jude. 'We could have a family holiday. Jude's parents want to meet us all.'

Charlie agreed to that idea. 'Sounds great.'

'Some of you can stay at mine. My parents bought the place from me, but they still class it as mine, so we're good to use it.' Jude looked at Harriet for confirmation. She nodded her approval and smiled widely. 'And I have a friend who owns a beach house not far from my place. He's never there and often lets people stay. I'll get that sorted for whoever doesn't stay with us. His house is huge. We could probably all fit.'

'That sounds lovely,' said Grace from the kitchen doorway. She moved closer when Charlie smiled her way, and he was happy to watch her curl up under his arm.

This is so perfect. Grace is doing good, we're renewing our vows, and we've arranged a family getaway. I haven't been to Malibu before, but it's just what the doctor ordered. This one.

Charlie's heart warmed as he looked around his hallway to see more of Grace's family join their circle, chatting about Malibu and how exciting it will be. Bryce offered to fly everyone there first-class, which caused even more excitement and only came to an abrupt halt when Lexi announced her waters had broken.

25

Grace

Sitting in Charlie's office on her own in the hospital, Grace stared out the window at the darkening sky. Lexi had not long given birth to a healthy baby girl and was doing well, Bryce had fallen asleep on his cousin Heath, dribbling down his top, whilst Ashley and Harrison took Fiona and Ronnie home. Kerri was already babysitting Harriet's son, Tommy, back at their parents' house, and Jude had taken Harriet out to get something to eat. Molly was asleep in a waiting room, resting on Freddy, and Charlie had been gone for twenty minutes. She was enjoying some alone time.

Muffled noises came from outside the office door every so often and people could be seen walking across the grass outside the window, probably heading home from visiting patients or having just finished a shift.

Aww, little baby April has joined our family. She's so adorable. I wish I had a baby. I wonder how badly I wanted one before I lost mine.

She hadn't asked Charlie about trying again. It might come across as weird, what with her not knowing him long, but part of her didn't want to wait. She was marrying him, she trusted him, and, apparently, they'd spent four happy years together. She'd always wanted lots of children. A big family like her own.

I hope they're all like their dad. Smart, funny, handsome, so respectful. I'll make sure they are. My sons won't be anything like Ewan. Argh! Get out of my head.

The door opened, and in walked Charlie, carrying a tray of food. 'How's my favourite person doing?'

'I'm good. Ooh, what have you got there?'

'Chicken and leek soup from the canteen. It's not bad. I got us some cheese toasties too. I checked on everyone. Those who are still here and awake have been fed and watered. Family is okay.'

Grace muffled her laugh with one hand. 'Thank you.'

Charlie pointed at the hot soup. 'Now, you get eating. You've had a long day up here, and, unlike me, you're not used to it.'

'When are you thinking of going back to work?'

He unwrapped the toasties and placed them on a napkin upon a saucer. 'When you're better.'

'I'm doing okay.'

He smiled as he bit into his food. 'Hmm, I know. Perhaps after our honeymoon. We'll see how you feel then.'

'Does that mean I get the all clear to go back to the Donkey Sanctuary?'

'Let's see what your doctor has to say about that.'

'I already called Dr Singh this morning. I was told I could go on honeymoon, so I'm guessing work should be okay. Besides, Red will probably only let me work part-time until she thinks I'm capable. She's the main doctor in my life.'

They laughed, and Grace tucked into her soup.

'Mmm, Charlie, this isn't bad at all.'

'One of the kitchen cooks makes this for the staff. She always saves me some if she knows I'm rostered on.'

'Oh, you're her favourite, are you?'

Charlie beamed a smile. 'Hey, I'm everyone's favourite.'

Grace laughed to herself as she mumbled, 'Hot Doc.'

Charlie tapped his chest. 'She's old enough to be my mother, and she says I remind her of her son.'

'Speaking of sons. I want to run something past you.' She paused, giving him room to speak, but he just waited for her to finish. 'Well, erm, I was wondering.' His eyebrows lifted as his eyes widened in anticipation. 'I want a baby.'

There. I said it, and he's smiling. And he's got that dreamy look in his eyes. My goodness, I love that look. He actually melts my heart into a pool of mush. Does he even know? Wow, I want him, right here next to the chicken and leek soup.

Grace couldn't help smiling at her own thoughts, which made his smile grow wider. 'Just out of curiosity, how many kids do you want?'

He gazed over her shoulder to peer out the window for a second. 'As many as you want.' He turned back to her and grinned. 'How many you thinking right now?'

'I'd like a big family. We have the room, and—'

'Hey, you don't have to convince me, honey. I'm ready when you are.'

'I'm ready now, Charlie.' She side-eyed the small sofa in his office.

Doesn't look too comfortable, but I don't really care.

She noticed him follow her eyes, and his sexy grin was back.

'You mean right now, Gracie?' He glanced at the lock on the door, causing Grace's stomach to do a double flip.

She swallowed hard. 'Erm, yes.'

Charlie went straight into doctor mode. 'I was thinking we should wait a while longer before going there. I want you to be sure about everything. And before you say it, I'm not trying to tell you about yourself. It just hasn't been that long since your accident, and you're already making huge changes in your life. Would you at least consider waiting till next year? See how you feel then. You might want to get a medical check before you come off the pill.'

'I know where you're coming from, but... Wait, I've haven't been taking any pills.'

'You were on the pill, Grace.'

She shook her head. 'I didn't know. No one said. I did wonder the first time we made love, but I... Oh, Charlie, I'm not going to lie to you, I did kind of brush it out of my mind, then I forgot about bringing it up. I wasn't scheming or anything, I—'

'Scheming? Gracie, you're my wife. If you want kids, we'll have kids. You know that. You wouldn't have to play those games with me. We spoke about having a family during our first year together. We made plans. You don't scheme. There's no need for you to anyway. We're a team, and we're in this together, and I've always given you whatever you want. Honey, please, don't worry about this. If you haven't been taking the pill, then, so what. I don't care. All I care about is you. I want you fit and healthy. Okay?'

Grace pulled in her lips and nodded.

Charlie sighed deeply. He got up and moved over to her side of his desk, lowering to his knees to rest his head on her lap. 'You could be pregnant now, Grace.'

She touched her stomach with one hand and placed the other on his head, raking her fingers into his hair. 'Would it be bad for the baby if I was? You know, because I'm not better yet.'

Charlie lifted his head. 'No. Your body is still a bit weak, but it's healthy enough. You just have memory loss, that's all.'

'I feel the need to apologise about the whole pill situation.'

'Well, don't. I told you, I don't care.'

'What if I'm pregnant already?'

'It's a bit early to do a test.'

'I haven't had a period since the accident, so I can't time anything.'

'Let's give it a couple more weeks, then do a test, if you want. We'll get a better result that way.'

'Meanwhile?'

'Meanwhile, what?'

'Do you want me to start taking the pill?'

Charlie creaked to a stand, took her hand, and led her to the sofa, making them both more comfortable. 'Let's wait till we find out if you're pregnant first.'

'I don't want to do anything wrong. I want to give our baby the best chance of survival.'

Charlie held both her hands whilst shaking his head slightly. 'There are never any guarantees, honey. You know that.'

'I do, but I still want to build up my body, take the right vitamins, feel more relaxed, that sort of thing.'

'You don't feel relaxed?'

She shrugged and lowered her eyes to their linked fingers. 'It's been a mad December, and it's not over yet. I know I'm rushing everything, trying to compact it all into this one month, but it's our month, isn't it? I want everything to be perfect for us. I want what I can't remember we had but know we had.' She breathed out a laugh and met his gentle eyes. 'I'm no good when it comes to patience, am I?'

He smiled, shaking his head. 'Nope.'

'I don't know. All I can tell you is how I feel. And I feel so very much in love with you. With us. It all just feels right. I know I was confused at first, but day by day, things keep improving. I remembered sausage rolls, for a start.' She smiled as he kissed her knuckles. 'It just feels right, Charlie,' she whispered, her voice cracking saying his name.

'That's how it was with us, Grace. Everything always felt so right. We knew we were blessed to have that kind of relationship, especially you, after all you had been through. I guess your soul knows it's safe with my soul, and that's what you're picking up on.'

Grace reached up and stroked over his jawline. 'I want all our babies to be just as beautiful as your soul, Charlie Wallis.'

He leaned his face into her hand. 'Me too.' He burst out laughing, and she slapped his shoulder. 'Come on, let's finish our food before it gets cold.'

'Nope.' Grace grabbed his shirt, tugging him towards her as she slanted backwards on the small sofa. 'I'm only hungry for you.'

'Oh, is that right? You want me right here?'

'I want you to practise getting me pregnant right here?'

Charlie laughed, pulled himself off her, quickly locked the door and closed the blinds, then joined her back on the sofa. 'Think I can handle that.'

Grace kissed him hard as soon as he was over her. She pulled back, taking in some air, and smiled. 'You do know that I won't be able to wait two more weeks to take a pregnancy test, right? I'll probably take one every day from now on.'

Charlie grinned as he stroked her hair away from her face. 'Yeah, I know. Good thing I can do them right here.'

'The only thing you need to be doing right here is this.' She reached down to unzip his jeans.

Charlie lifted his weight to help her undress him.

'Hey, Charlie, have we ever made love in here before?'

'Nope,' he mumbled in between kisses on her neck. 'First time.'

Grace pushed him away. 'Wait, Charlie. My head's in a whirl.'

He sat up quickly, concern flashing across his eyes. 'You need water?'

'No, not like that. I mean, I want to do a test right now. I can't think straight.'

Charlie stood, zipping his jeans. 'Give me two secs.'

She watched him whizz out the room, and true to his word, he was back before she had time to think.

He pointed out the door. 'Go next door and pee in the cup.'

The toilet was dull and sterile and not the happiest of places to find out her news. Grace was glad to get back to the cosiness of Charlie's office, which only felt that way because he was there. She watched him dip something into her urine, then followed his eyes as they made their way back to her.

Am I really ready to be pregnant? It's a bit soon, but tough if I am. I'll happily get on with it, but maybe it would be for the best if we did wait till next year, once I'm feeling stronger. My memory might have come back by then. I hope it does. I hope...

'It's negative, Grace, but it's probably because it's too soon to tell.'

Something inside of her deflated more than she thought it would at a negative result. Charlie's arms were suddenly around her, holding her back close to his chest. His mouth pressed down onto her head.

'I'm okay, Charlie. I don't think I'm pregnant anyway. And it's best we wait till my body gets back to some sort of normal routine. All the stress is messing with me.'

'You sure you're okay?'

She turned in his arms and gave him a peck on the lips. 'I'm sure. I just got carried away for a moment from all the buzz of April being born. I can think clearly now.'

'If you want, we can still skip the pill, make love whenever we want, and if it happens before we're fully ready, then it happens.'

Grace smiled and kissed him again. 'Yes, I think I'm going to enjoy practising.'

'You see, we know how to make plans, Even the ones where the plans can just make themselves. Hey, Gracie, we're gonna have loads of kids one day. It'll happen. You want to get back to having a go right now?'

'Honestly, Charlie. I don't actually want to think about babies while we're making love. I just want to think about us. Like you said, if it happens, then it happens, but let's not concentrate on that part. Let's just be us, doing what we enjoy. Being together. And I really do enjoy being with you. In every sense.'

He nudged her nose with his own, then kissed the base of her neck. 'I'm right there with you, honey. Now, let's make some memories in my office.' He glanced up to look around him. 'You know, I'll think of this every time I'm in here from now on. I won't be able to concentrate.'

Grace giggled and tugged him closer. 'Ooh, I like that you'll have that memory of me. We'd better make it a good one.'

26

Charlie

Charlie paced in his parents' hotel suite, answering numerous questions fired at him from his mother. He didn't have all the answers she wanted. All he could tell her was what he already knew. Grace was doing fine. Yes, the wedding was her idea. No, she doesn't remember anything yet.

He thought about the little things that had passed through her head on occasion. Dr Singh had told him during a private chat that things were looking hopeful and to try not to worry too much.

That was way easier said than done. All Charlie did was stress over his wife. He failed to mention Ewan to his family, knowing it wouldn't help matters.

Charlene pulled a comb through her dark pixie cut, then brushed the back of her husband's shoulders with her hand, wiping away some fluff. 'I'm so glad we're here now, Charlie. We've been so worried about Grace, and more so about you.'

His dad glanced over his shoulder as his wife stepped away from her fussing. 'How you holding up, son?'

Charlie shrugged, not feeling the need to talk about Grace's condition once again. Part of him wanted to forget it existed and just return to a normal life with her. That seemed doable, especially now she was loving him again.

I really don't know what I would have done if she'd walked away.

He swallowed hard, then bent to hand his mother her shoes. 'It might be a bit hectic round Fiona's. The whole family are there, organising. There isn't much left to do, as Harrison had the Christmas Eve party covered.' He inhaled a deep breath, loosening his tight lungs.

'I have an idea, Peter.' Charlene nudged her husband's arm just as he was about to take a sip of water from a bottle. He wiped his mouth and frowned her way. 'Charlie and Grace can come stay with us for a while.'

Peter seemed okay with the suggestion, but Charlie wasn't so sure.

'She needs to be around everything that's familiar. Plus, she loves Waterside Cottage. I think it's finally starting to feel like her home.'

Charlene tied the lace on her pumps. 'I think a change of scenery would be good for her. Sometimes, that works too.'

'We're going to Lapland for a week soon. That will give us a break.'

A trip away will do Grace some good. Things can only get better from now on. I have to believe we're over the worst.

Charlie followed his parents down to the lobby, where his brother and sister were waiting. William and Amy asked the same questions about Grace his parents had, and Charlie was starting to feel exhausted. Given the chance, he'd go home, curl up in bed with his wife, and hold on to her forever.

He needed a break himself. He did everything he could think of to get his wife to come back to him. And it seemed to have worked, so now was not the time to crumble.

Stop worrying. Life may not be perfect, but this is where we're at, and this is just fine. Everything is fine. I just need to keep reminding myself.

Throughout the car ride over to the Hadleys', Charlie felt rattled. He couldn't quite put his finger on what was bothering him. He told himself over and over that things were working out, that Grace was okay, and their new life together was going to be just as wonderful as their old one.

Grace gave him the biggest hug after greeting his family as soon as they entered her family home. Charlie couldn't help but beam. Everything about her always made him smile. The dancing snowman on her Christmas jumper added to his joy.

He shook off the negative vibes swirling in his mind as he shrugged off his jacket.

Grace cornered him by the coat rack by the door. 'I love that everyone is together.' She stroked her hand low on his back and gave him a cheeky grin.

'You want to take me to your old room?' he whispered, peppering kisses behind her ear.

She cupped his face and kissed his mouth. 'I want to take you everywhere.'

He looked deeply into the dreamy blue eyes sparkling his way. 'I'm so glad you found me again, Grace. I...' He tried to say more but his voice broke.

Grace's brow crinkled as she tipped her head closer to his. 'Hey, it's okay.' She took his hand and quickly guided him upstairs to her old bedroom she used to share with Ashley. 'Sit here a moment.'

He plopped down on her single bed and turned to face her as she joined his side. 'Sorry, Grace. I'm okay.'

'No, you're not. This has been a huge trauma for you too. You're the one who received the call that your wife had been mowed down by a car and left for dead. You're the one who had to watch me day after day, night after night, lying in a hospital bed, in a coma. You're the one who had to deal with the love of your life not remembering you. Charlie, my lovely, this has all been a lot for you as well. It's okay if you have a moment where you cry, or scream.' She breathed out a quiet laugh and nudged his elbow with her own.

'Sometimes I feel like yelling.'

Grace nodded and snuggled closer to his side. 'I get that.'

'This isn't about me though. It's about you and what you've been through.'

Squeezing his hand gently, she shook her head. 'That's where you're wrong. This is about us. We're a team. What happens to one of us, happens to us both. Of course this is going to affect you too. Blimming heck, love, you're only human.'

'You sounded like your mother then.'

They smiled at each other, then hugged until their sides ached and they had to straighten their bodies.

'Charlie, I honestly think everything is going to be okay now. You took me on my Christmas journey. We went to the past. We had the present, and now we're going to create a future. Scrooge has been reborn.' She pointed to the doorway. 'I feel the need to buy the biggest goose.'

Charlie laughed and clamped his hand over hers on his lap. 'Oh, honey, I just wish that none of this happened to us.'

'We need to count our blessings. It will help if we only focus on the good stuff.'

'Yeah, I know.' Charlie took a breath and sat up tall. 'All right, I'm ready to look only at the future.'

Grace pushed him backwards on the bed and leaned over him. 'I like our future. It has lots of Christmases in it, that much I do know.'

Charlie pulled her face down to meet his. 'And lots of kisses.'

She giggled on his lips, and he absorbed the light vibration along with the strawberry lip gloss she was wearing. 'I'm going to keep kissing you right here until my mum calls us downstairs. We can pretend we're teenagers, without a care in the world.'

'When you're kissing me, I don't have a care in the world.'

Grace pulled away and smiled. 'Were we always this soppy?'

He scrunched his nose and gave a slight nod. 'Yeah.'

'I think I love us, you know.'

'Hey, what's not to love?' He pulled her back to his mouth before she could add to his comment. Within a moment, Charlie had completely forgotten exactly where they were, that their whole family was downstairs, and that the bedroom door was wide open. He had one hand under her jumper, and the other was tucked into the top of her unfastened jeans.

Their heated kissing session wasn't about to cool down anytime soon. Grace's hand raked through his hair whilst her other hand pressed his backside further towards her.

Charlie was slipping away into her realm. Falling deeper and deeper, with nothing beneath him. The Northern Lights were back, swirling overhead, and red tinsel wrapped around their bodies, holding them together. The smell of cinnamon filled the air as bells chimed and Christmas music began to play quietly in the distance.

He returned to the Santa booth. To her gorgeous face. The smell of peppermint coming from her mouth. The way her eyes twinkled with surprise.

Grace wrapped her legs around his waist, pulling him tighter, and Charlie snapped out of his trance. Their kiss deepened, and their clothes were about to come off.

'Oi,' called Ashley, standing in the doorway. 'Get a room. And I don't mean my old one.'

Grace moved away from Charlie, straightening her dishevelled hair, and he couldn't help but warm at the slight blush on her cheeks and just how plump her lips looked. He followed her up to sit more appropriately on the bed.

Harrison peered over Ashley's shoulder and laughed. 'Teenagers!' he mocked. 'You've always got to keep your eye on them.'

Grace pointed their way. 'Erm, and why are you two up here? I bet you were going to snog on Ashley's old bed. Hmm?'

Ashley looked far from convincing as she furrowed her brow whilst shaking her head. 'No, we weren't.'

'Liar,' mumbled Grace, standing and taking Charlie's hand. 'Come on, my lovely. Let's give them their teenager moment.'

Ashley went to protest again, but Harrison tugged her towards her bed, which still held two teddy bears and a stuffed hippo.

'Might as well, while we're here, Ash,' he whispered close to her ear, making her side-eye Grace and Charlie over by the door.

Grace pulled Charlie back into the bedroom, then pulled out a game from under her bed. 'Or we could play Kerplunk.'

Harrison laughed as Ashley frowned, not looking as keen as him to play Grace's old game.

Charlie was already sitting on the floor, with his back against the bed. 'Come on. This will be fun.'

Grace gave him a wink, then set up the game whilst Ashley reluctantly sat cross-legged on the floor next to Harrison, who was grinning more than anyone.

Charlie relaxed, enjoying his company, completely ready for new beginnings. His wife was letting him know the future was going to be filled with lots more laughter, family time, and love.

27

Grace

Molly was the first to spin the bottle on the floor in the living room of Waterside Cottage. It stopped, pointing at Ashley, who slumped her shoulders and sighed dramatically.

'Oh, come on. I can't even believe we're playing this.'

Kerri laughed as she nudged her arm. 'You're only moaning because it landed on you.'

'Well, I'm not doing one of your stupid dares, Kel,' said Ashley, huffing.

Kerri clapped her hands together in front of her chest. 'Ooh, truth it is.'

'I've got one,' said Harriet, flapping one hand her way. 'Is it true you snogged Wade in the back of the burger bar?'

Ashley choked on the mouthful of white wine she had just gulped. 'No, it's bloody not. Who's been saying that? I hate the man's guts. I hated him when we were kids too, and anyone else who hung out with Viktor.'

Grace's orange juice went down the wrong hole, as she laughed along with her sisters.

'He loved you,' sang out Molly, opting for a high-pitched tone.

Ashley raised her brow as she uncurled her crossed legs. 'I don't want to talk about any of Vik's friends, thanks. You do know he's still mates with Viktor, right? Vik tried to destroy Harrison, Grace, and me.' She turned to Grace to speak, but Grace raised one hand.

'Don't say sorry again, Ash. It wasn't your fault. We can't keep going over this.'

'But you would be fine if it wasn't for Vik. He only paid someone to knock you down to get back at me. I had no idea he would go that far.'

'I'm fine, Ash. My memory will come back. Please stop blaming yourself. I need you to, okay?'

Ashley nodded whilst clenching her fists. 'Okay, but I still wish I could smack him one.'

'Did you ever hit Bryce?' asked Lexi. 'He always seems wary around you.'

'No. It's not my fault your fiancé is scared of me.'

Kerri scoffed. 'All our partners are scared of you, Ash.' She glanced around the circle of sisters. 'Can't think why,' she teased.

Ashley sipped her wine. 'Again, not my fault.'

Grace leaned into her. 'Aww, leave our Ash alone. She's not so tough. Harrison broke through her prickly vines.'

'Actually,' said Ashley, grinning, 'I chatted him up. Harrison is the shy, reserved type.'

'He probably can't get a word in with you.' Molly flicked a crisp her way, which Ashley picked up and ate.

Harriet leaned forward to spin the bottle. 'Erm, let's not forget this is Lexi's first time out since giving birth, so no dares for her.'

'Aww, thanks, sis, but I'm okay.' Lexi glanced at her lime-infused water. 'I've left Bryce with enough breast milk to last a week, and I'm only here overnight. Ooh, Gracie, are you excited for the wedding tomorrow?'

Grace couldn't believe Christmas Eve was upon them already. One moment, December felt as though it had flown by, and the next, as though it had gone on forever. She couldn't wait to see Charlie the next day. She was so excited to renew their wedding vows on their makeshift wedding day.

'I feel okay, Lex. It's a bit weird if I overthink the whole situation, so I'm trying to take each step as it comes.'

'I like Charlie,' said Kerri. 'He's always come across as lovely. You should have seen the state of him when you were in a coma. Whoa, he was bad for the first week.'

I probably would have crumbled into a thousand pieces. He's so much stronger than me, coping with all that.

Molly tapped Kerri's knee. 'Let's not talk about the sad stuff the night before Gracie's big day, eh, Kel? Look, the bottle is pointing at Harriet.'

Lexi grinned as Harriet announced she wasn't doing a dare. 'Okay, Hal. You and Jude are always in the sea. So, have you ever gone all the way in the motion of the ocean?'

Ashley laughed out loud. 'That's her business.' She turned to Harriet. 'But now it's out there... Well?'

Harriet turned a slight shade of pink. 'Might have. Spin the bottle.'

The women laughed as Kerri swirled the empty bottle of lemonade around.

'How's the new house coming along, Hal?' asked Grace, remembering to keep up with family news.

'Getting there. I'll be glad when it's fully built and we can settle in. It's a bit of a tight squeeze in the caravan, but our Tommy loves it. He's treating it like a holiday.'

'And your new business?'

Harriet smiled warmly at Grace. 'That's doing okay. We'll pick up more come spring, what with it being mostly water sports, but Jude's wetsuit line is selling well, and I'm still doing some shifts at the hotel. Do you remember any of my story with Jude?'

'No, sorry. But you look happy, and that's all that matters.'

Harriet beamed from ear to ear. 'I am. I love Jude so much. I can't believe he came into my life.'

'I feel that way about Bryce,' said Lexi. 'I know we went to school together, but to have him come home and, well, it's just lovely that it worked out for us in the end.'

Grace's heart warmed as she looked at each of her sisters in turn. They were all so happy. She was glad she could now be part of their club. 'When are you going to get married, Lex?'

'We wanted to wait till the baby was born before we set a date. So next year, hopefully. Bryce wants us to get married on a beach somewhere abroad, but I don't know. As long as my whole family can be there, I don't care where it happens.'

Kerri pulled the bowl of popcorn onto her lap. 'Toby says we'll marry once he's finished with school. Not sure how many more years that will be. It takes forever to become a doctor.'

'I'm going to propose to Harrison on New Year's Eve. I knew I was going to marry him from the beginning. He'll say a very shy yes, then kiss me till we need to breathe.' Ashley laughed. 'Once we get a licence to hold weddings at the castle, we'll get married there.'

Grace had to laugh. 'Oh, you have it all figured out. What about Harrison, doesn't he get a say?'

'Harrison will love it, trust me. I wouldn't do anything I thought he might hate. When someone's not very vocal, you have to learn how to read them. I know when he likes something.'

Molly scoffed, flapping her hand. 'We don't want to know about your sex life, Ash.'

Harriet frowned. 'Wanted to know about mine though.'

Grace pointed at the bottle. 'Go on, Molly. Truth or dare?'

'I'm going for truth as well. It seems to be the theme tonight.'

Ashley rubbed her chin as her eyes filled with mischief. 'Hmm, let me see. What can we ask our Molly that will embarrass her?'

'Erm, I don't get embarrassed as easily as you lot. Well, except when I trip over in the street and fall flat on my face. That's where my embarrassment sits. So if you want details about Freddy, I'm happy to share.'

Grace scoffed. 'I don't think he will be.'

Molly had to agree with that. 'True. Best not then. Moving on…'

'Hey, wait a minute.' Ashley stretched out one leg to tap Molly's knee with her foot. 'You haven't answered a question yet?'

'Okay. Hit me.'

'I know,' said Kerri, 'when Grace woke up in hospital, thinking she was still with Freddy Morland, how did that make you feel?'

Lexi shook her head. 'Don't cause trouble.'

'I'm just asking.'

Molly huffed and rolled her dark eyes. 'I was just worried about Grace, that's all.'

'I still can't believe you dated Freddy, Grace,' said Ashley, about to swallow the dregs of her drink.

'Oi, what's wrong with my Freddy?' snapped Molly. 'He's lovely, I'll have you know.'

Grace nodded. 'Freddy is lovely. We were just two friends trying to help each other, I guess. We didn't even sleep together.'

Molly wrinkled her nose. 'I don't think I would have got with Freddy if you had. He told me about you two way back when, but it's always a little weird. I'm just glad it was a flash in the pan and nothing more.'

Grace smiled her way. 'He loves you very much, Molls.'

Molly smiled back. 'I know. It's all good.'

'So, Grace,' said Kerri. 'How long did it take you to fall back in love with Charlie? Was it as soon as Ashley moved out?'

'I'm not sure. He kept showing me how much he loved me. He took me out and about. Gave me a Christmas to remember, and things started to feel familiar about him. It didn't take long at all, really.' She raised her hands to gesture to the room. 'Obviously. Look at me. I'm sitting in my home that I share with him, waiting to renew our vows tomorrow, then we're having a big family dinner on Christmas up at the castle, then we're going on our honeymoon. I don't think my heart ever stopped loving him.'

'Our hearts are a lot stronger than our minds, aren't they?' said Lexi, rubbing over her deflated pregnancy bump.

'I used to think my heart was an idiot,' said Harriet. 'But now I kind of like the way it operates. It knew Jude was safe. I swear my soul took one look at him and said, *about time you showed up.*'

Grace smiled at them all. 'I'm glad you're all settled and happy. Ever since I was a kid, all I wanted was a relationship like Mum and Dad's. We've been lucky, you know. Not everyone gets to grow up in a loving family, with happy parents, and lots of onions.'

Everyone burst out laughing.

Lexi had tears in her eyes. 'Oh my goodness, Bryce came home with a bag of onions last week. He couldn't stop laughing. Said he didn't know what to say to Dad.'

Ashley took a breath, regaining her composure. 'Harrison's got one on the kitchen windowsill. Dad told him to put it there. So he did. He didn't even ask why. He's so polite.'

'Oh, I love our dad,' said Harriet, clutching her top.

Everyone agreed and continued to chatter away about how wonderful and somewhat odd their parents were, leaving Grace to her thoughts.

She felt so incredibly blessed. All those years spent with Ewan, she knew she didn't fit with him. Her family taught her what love looked like. She should have left him as soon as she felt he wasn't right. She was so proud of herself for leaving in the end. Now she had everything that made her heart sing with joy.

I have this crazy mob, a beautiful home, and the best man in the world loving me. I'm getting married tomorrow. In a castle. Ooh, I bloody love my life. I love you too, Charlie Wallis. I hope you can feel my energy. I'm sending it all your way. Roll on Christmas Eve. It's going to be the most perfect day.

28

Charlie

The grey-stone, walk-in fireplace, with its red-brick top, crackled in the black grate, helping to illuminate the thick green-and-gold wallpaper and shiny dark flooring of the second biggest room at Castle on the Mead. Ornate chairs, each decorated with a big red bow, lined either side of the large but cosy space, leaving a walkway down the middle.

Charlie and Grace stood at the front, holding hands whilst smiling at their seated guests. Ashley was playing the part of the officiant, which started with her telling everyone to shush.

'Charlie and Grace are going to renew their vows now, so no flash photography, and turn your phones off. We haven't got long before the paying guests for the Christmas Eve party turn up. So no interruptions.'

'Very romantic, Ash,' called Molly, snuggling up to Freddy.

Ashley flapped her hands down. 'Charlie would like to speak first.' She gave him a slight nod, then took a step back.

Charlie felt all eyes on him and was pretty sure he wasn't as nervous at their proper wedding. He couldn't take his eyes off Grace, absorbing every part of her, so much so, he hardly heard Ashley.

My God, how beautiful she looks in that long red dress. I love her hair pulled up like that, and I'm especially gonna love it later tonight in bed when I get to unravel it in my fingers. Oh, Grace, you really have no idea just how much I love you.

Ashley dramatically cleared her throat, bringing him out of his trance with his wife.

'Grace, we've been through a lot over the past four years, but we stayed strong. Loving each other. Sticking around when the chips were down. You always had my back. I couldn't ask for a better team player. The one thing being around you taught me is that I have the ability to love unconditionally. In among all my fears and worries, a part of me knew you would come back to me, somehow. Our love has always been way too strong. Nothing can touch us, honey. I vow, just as I did on our wedding day, to be by your side here and among the stars. I love you, Gracie. You're all my Christmases rolled into one.'

Fiona wiped a tear away as Kerri clapped, then stopped when no one else joined in. Charlie gave her a smile, then waited to hear what Grace had to say.

'Well, Hot Doc. What can I say about you? Trust me, I've been up half the night trying to find the right words, and I still can't think of anything that does you justice.' She lowered her eyes for a moment, and Charlie touched her chin, regaining her focus. 'I know I forgot about you. Us. But something inside me always felt safe around you. I guess, my soul knew you even if my brain didn't. I've been confused a lot lately, but you kept bringing me back home. Creating stability and warmth. I just fell in love with you a little bit more every hour of every day. The past has gone now, Charlie, but we've got a whole future ahead of us, and I'm looking forward to being together. I love you. Thank you for my memories.'

It was Ronnie's turn to casually swipe a tear from his cheek.

The room fell silent until Harrison gave Ashley a nod, reminding her to speak.

Ashley jolted out of her dreamy trance. 'Oh, yeah. So, Charlie, you may now place the ring on Grace's finger.'

Grace looked surprised. 'What ring? I didn't know we were doing rings.'

Charlie pulled out the platinum band Harrison had made. 'You always wanted one that was another colour from gold.' He slipped it onto her bare wedding finger. 'Now, you have choices.' He was happy to see her beam down at her new accessory.

Oh, Gracie, I think this is our most magical Christmas yet.

He stole a look at her smiling parents, then turned back to his bride.

'Thank you, Charlie. I love it so much.'

He lifted her hand and tenderly kissed her new ring.

'Wish you well to wear it, love,' said Fiona as Grace flashed her ring out to their audience.

Ashley flapped one hand towards her mother, shushing her and placing her back into her seat, as she was about to get up. 'We're not finished yet, Mum.' She turned back to the happy couple and smiled. 'Charlie and Grace Wallis, I now pronounce you husband and wife. Again. You may kiss.'

Everyone cooed as Charlie dipped Grace slightly and placed his lips upon hers.

'Now can I clap?' asked Kerri.

Lexi nodded. 'Yay!'

The Hadley and Wallis families joined in with the cheering, clapping, and throwing of red, green, and white pieces of confetti.

Charlie watched Grace hug her best friend, Vivien, knowing his wife was happy Vivien's partner wasn't there.

He remembered that Grace didn't like him and was glad the policeman was on duty.

The room was filled only with love. He didn't want to entertain anyone Grace wasn't comfortable with, so the atmosphere was alive and as noisy as it usually was when all the Hadleys were together.

He held Grace's hand as they left the room to enter the main hall, where the buffet lined two walls, the DJ was ready to play his tunes, and the raffle stall held all of Grace's hampers.

The DJ played 'Tiny Dancer' and Grace went into her interpretive dance, making Charlie roar with laughter. He quickly grabbed her by the waist and swirled her around and into his chest, where he held her tightly, placing her head on his shoulder.

'Charlie, this is the best Christmas Eve ever.'

'And you are the best wife ever.' He pulled away slightly so he could look into her eyes.

'We're lucky, aren't we?'

'Yeah, honey. We are.'

Grace giggled as she gestured towards the Santa booth in the corner of the room. 'Shall we get a picture?'

'Come on then.'

Grace took his hand and pulled him through the others dancing. They entered the booth, sat down, and breathed out a laugh in each other's direction.

Charlie kissed her just as the shot was taken, delighting in how she looked.

She reached up to stroke over his cheek, revealing her love for him within her eyes. 'Who needs mistletoe!' She kissed him hard, almost climbing on top of his lap.

Charlie laughed on her lips and mumbled, 'Speaking of mistletoe.'

Grace pulled back. 'What?'

'Come with me.' Charlie led her out to the back garden, where her favourite donkey stood waiting with Sidney and Red.

'Oh my goodness.' Grace quietly clapped her hands together before hugging Mistletoe, who seemed to enjoy the attention.

'We're not staying,' said Red. 'Got to get this one back, but your old man there thought it would be nice for you to have a wedding selfie with Mistletoe.'

Grace turned as Charlie handed her one of her small cameras.

'Knock yourself out.' He watched patiently, then joined in with the photos when asked, avoiding any jealous nips coming his way from the protective donkey.

Grace pressed Charlie up against the castle wall once Sidney and Red had left to take Mistletoe home. She kissed his mouth, then cheek, then trailed down to his neck, nuzzling her nose into the collar of his white shirt. 'We could just sneak off home, you know,' she mumbled on his skin.

Sounds good to me, but...

'Later, Grace. Let's get back to the party. The guests have arrived, and we promised Ashley and Harrison we'd help out with the raffle prizes.'

'Ooh, did you buy any tickets?'

'Only for the Black Crow Alley one.'

'Lovely. Fingers crossed, eh.'

Grace went to head inside, but Charlie pulled her back into his hold. She shivered, as light snowflakes began to fall, so he wrapped his arms around her shoulders and kept her cheek close to his own. 'One more moment, Mrs Wallis.'

Grace's lips curled on his skin. 'We have all the moments, Charlie.'

But it could have all been so different. I could have lost you in the accident. I could have never shared another moment with you again.

He squeezed her a little tighter.

'It's okay, Charlie. I'm safe.'

He lightly placed a kiss on her head, then followed her back inside, where they parted ways to mingle.

The music was pumping, champagne was flowing, the main hall was alive with people wearing Christmas hats and tinsel, and Harrison and Ashley looked over the moon.

I'm glad this place is working out for them. They deserve... No way! What's he doing here?

Charlie looked over the top of Jude's shoulder to glare at Ewan, who was standing by the sausage roll wedding cake. Jude and Bryce were talking about something, but Charlie's focus was on the man who did nothing but make Grace suffer. His heart started to pump harder, so he relaxed his clenched fingers and took a calming breath.

Grace was chatting happily to her friends from the Tuesday Club, with the exception of Ewan. Charlie wasn't sure if she had noticed his arrival yet.

What the actual... He totally just ate one of our wedding cake sausage rolls! I don't think it's possible for me to hate him any more than I already do.

Harrison tapped his shoulder, breaking his glare with Ewan. 'Hey, stop with the death stare. You're a doctor. If anything happens to him, you're obliged to help.'

Charlie shook his head at Harrison's attempt to lighten his mood. 'Every time I see him, I just want to donate his body to science. While he's still alive.'

Harrison breathed out a laugh, then pulled Charlie out to the hallway. 'Take a moment. Don't let anything ruin your big day.'

A few deep breaths later, and Charlie started to calm down. 'You're right. I shouldn't let his presence spoil anything. Grace already told me the next time he tries to speak to her, she's going to tell him to go away. She's got it covered. I need to back off. He just grinds on me.'

'Yeah, I know. There are loads of people here tonight. You can easily avoid him. It's only a few hours.'

'He wasn't invited. Grace told her Tuesday Club friends she wouldn't be going to their meet-up in the pub today, then she invited them to join our evening. I guess he thought that meant him too.'

'Maybe. Or maybe he had already bought a ticket to the Christmas Eve party we're hosting.'

Charlie shook his head slightly. 'Yeah, I forgot about that for a moment.' He rubbed the back of his stiff neck. 'I can't believe it's Christmas tomorrow. This has been the strangest month of my life.'

'But it worked out in the end.'

'I guess. Grace is settled now, so that's good. She seems happy. We've made a lot of progress.'

'That's Christmas for you. The time for miracles.'

Charlie gestured towards the main hall. 'It would be a miracle if I walk back in there and Ewan has disappeared.'

'Well, that's one thing to ask Santa for. Speaking of which, come on, it's time to draw the raffles. Ashley will start getting stressed if we don't do it at the allocated timeslot.' He laughed along with Charlie. 'Why did I get the mad sister?'

'Oi, I heard that.' Ashley floated over in her long green dress, and Harrison drew her in for a kiss.

And that's my cue to leave.

Without interrupting their embrace, Charlie made his way back to the main event, rummaging around in his pocket for his raffle ticket. He glanced around for Grace, wanting to stand by her side when the lucky winners were announced, but she was nowhere to be seen.

He asked Harriet if she'd seen Grace, but she hadn't. Neither had any of the others. He caught Lexi coming back from the bathroom, but she said Grace wasn't in there.

I can't see Vivien. Maybe they're outside.

He walked through the kitchen to get to the back garden, but no one was out there. It was dark and snowing, but the grounds were alight with fairy lights and large colourful Christmas ornaments. Charlie went to go back inside but stopped when he thought he heard a voice in the distance. Tipping his head to one side, he closed his eyes and listened carefully. After a minute, the sound came again.

That's Grace shouting.

Charlie sprinted across the lawn, heading in the direction of the muffled noises. As he got closer to the bridge, he could see Grace and Ewan in some sort of scuffle.

'Grace!' he yelled.

Grace turned at the same time Ewan let go of the hold he had on her.

It all seemed to happen in slow motion.

Charlie felt as though his feet were stuck in quicksand, pulling him under, stopping him from getting to where he needed to be as Grace slipped backwards and toppled over the side of the bridge, banged her head on a large rock below, and disappeared under the lake.

Ewan had already scarpered by the time life poured back into Charlie's body, waking every particle of him as the icy liquid burned his lungs.

Frantically searching beneath the waterline, it took what seemed like forever but was less than a minute to find Grace and bring her back to the surface. Charlie pulled her out of the lake, checked her vitals, swiped his hand over her bleeding head wound, then checked his phone, praying it would still work.

It didn't.

Grace was breathing and no bones were broken, so Charlie picked her up and carried her back to the castle.

Kerri was the first to see them coming. She quickly called an ambulance as Charlie rushed into the emptiness of the study to place Grace upon a brown sofa.

'Grace. Grace.'

She wasn't responding. He took the phone from Kerri, whilst she went to tell her parents, and told the operator everything he knew. He ripped one of the cushion covers off and pressed it against the bleeding wound. Grace was out cold, and Charlie needed to get her to hospital. He was all set to move her to his car when he heard the sirens.

Fiona and Ronnie perched at her feet as Molly cried out for answers.

Charlie's head was in such a whirl, he was struggling to be in doctor mode, let alone talk about what he had witnessed on the bridge, but he told them, then quickly relayed Grace's condition to the two female medics entering the room. Within minutes, Grace was transferred to the ambulance, with Charlie by her side, trying to take charge. Trying to get his head back in the game.

The Hadleys weren't far behind, jumping in cars, forgetting Christmas Eve existed at all. Jude and Bryce stayed behind to help clear out the partygoers with Vivien, who was on the warpath, searching the grounds for Ewan. Very soon it was as though the castle had never had a party there at all.

Charlie rested his head on Grace's hand as the ambulance whizzed to the hospital.

Wake up, Gracie. Please wake up.

29

Grace

Hot Doc: **Thank you for the most perfect date. Do you want to have lunch with me tomorrow? There's a coffee shop just by the hospital. They do nice sandwiches. I only have a forty minute break, but I'd like to spend that time with you. What do you say, Grace? You game?**

Grace: **Hello again, Charlie. You only left me five minutes ago. I haven't even had a chance to take my boots off. Are you missing me already?**

Hot Doc: **I just want to book another date with you before anyone tries.**

Grace: **There is no one else. And yes, I would love to meet you for coffee shop sandwiches. But you have to wear a Santa hat. It's December, after all.**

Hot Doc: **Deal. But you have to wear one too. Okay?**

Grace: **I'm going to wear the one I bought at the Sandly Christmas Market.**

Hot Doc: **I still regret not asking you out that day.**

Grace: **Never mind. I'll see you tomorrow. I'm just going to remove some sliced onions from my dad's record player, then I'm going to bed. My nephew put onions in** his shoes last week. Let that be a warning to you for the day you get to meet my family.

Hot Doc: **I look forward to meeting the Hadleys. Goodnight, Grace. Sleep well. x**

* * *

Grace's head hurt, and she felt cold. She looked around Black Crow Alley, wondering why she was standing alone outside Mama's Love. There wasn't anyone else around, and all the shops were closed, except one.

A dull wall light barely lit the doorway at the top of three steps flanked by two five-foot Nutcrackers.

A faint whiff of cinnamon wafted towards her, raising her nose, encouraging her feet to move.

Tentatively, Grace entered the premises to find the signless shop was a toy store. The vibrant colours and musical chimes brought the smallest of smiles to her face.

'Hello,' said a deep voice.

She turned to see a snowman wave one hand her way, so she did what she thought was polite and waved back.

The four-foot snowman chuckled and wiggled his hips from side to side to the beat of the clinking music. 'Do you remember me, Grace?'

'No,' she just about managed, as her throat felt clogged from surprise alone.

'You made me in Lapland.'

Grace scanned his red scarf. 'I did?'

'Do you remember the song we sang that day?'

She thought for a moment, then nodded. 'Yes. It was "Let it Snow" and Charlie kept laughing all the way through. We ended up in a snowball fight, then we went inside to warm up and... Well, you don't need to know the rest.'

The snowman was still happily dancing away. 'Come to the back of the shop. I want to show you something.' He jiggled and wiggled his way down an aisle, and Grace couldn't help but bob her head as she followed.

The most beautiful ornate wardrobe she had ever seen was perched against the back wall. Its dark polished wood and poking out feet gleamed just as much as all the toys she passed along the way.

The snowman turned the brass key and opened both doors to reveal a mixture of coats upon a rail. He waved her forward. 'Come. Look.'

Grace side-eyed him as she approached. She reached out to a soft dark-green jacket that looked like one Charlie owned. She slid it to one side because a bright light had appeared at the back of the wardrobe, and she needed to see what it was.

'Go on,' said the snowman.

Without looking back, she stepped inside the wardrobe, moved through the coats, and found herself entering a snow-covered forest. She quickly turned to ask the snowman if she was in Narnia, but the wardrobe had disappeared. 'Hey, where did you go?'

No one answered. No one was there but her. Light snowflakes fell, and suddenly Grace didn't feel so cold anymore. The snow was soft and slightly crunchy, and the evergreens around her sparkled to life, changing into Christmas trees, fully decorated with ornaments and baubles. Carollers started singing 'Good King Wenceslas' somewhere in the distance, and a beautiful reindeer slowly walked past, stopping only for a second to glance her way before entering the trees.

Grace could hear the jingle jangle of bells as a husky-drawn sleigh came to a halt in front of her. There wasn't a driver to steer the six dogs, making her wonder if they had fallen off along the trail.

'Get on,' said the lead dog, in a gruff voice. His two different colour irises gleamed as a sparkle flashed from his sharp teeth.

Tucking herself beneath the thick blue blanket in the sleigh, Grace braced herself for the journey.

'Look up, Grace,' said the lead dog.

The Northern Lights swirled in and out of the sky. The different shades of green danced before Grace's wide eyes, causing her heart to smile way more than her mouth.

'Whoa!' she whispered, snuggling further into the sled as the sky continued to glow.

'Do you remember this place, Grace?' asked the husky.

She nodded and silently mouthed the word, 'Yes.'

* * *

The cream satin and lace on her long dress made her feel as though she were wearing a million pounds. Her eyes slipped down slowly over her reflection in the tall floor mirror, from her satin shoes to the diamond tiara upon her pulled-up blonde locks. Her mum told her it was time, so she left the large bedroom to hook arms with her dad outside.

Charlie looked dapper, she thought as she floated towards his warm smile. His hand was shaking slightly, so she squeezed his fingers gently, letting him know everything was fine. Their eyes met, Charlie blinking back tears, and Grace wanted nothing more than to kiss him.

Muffled voices were around her, but she couldn't tell if they were trying to gain her attention. Only Charlie had her attention. She was focused on those beautiful midnight eyes sparkling only for her. She swore she could see the actual moon within them. A bright full moon that told her a story of magic and mystery. One that made her believe in the wildest of dreams and the happiest of places.

Charlie placed his lips upon hers, giving her a tender kiss that told the best story of all. Their love story.

'Do you remember this moment, Grace?' he whispered in her ear.

'Always,' she whispered back.

'I will love you for always. You give me life.'

'You have given me everything I ever dreamed of, Charlie. I never knew this much happiness existed until I met you. You are life. You're everything, and I will love you forever.'

'Come on, Grace. Let's go ice skating now.'

She giggled whilst giving her dress the once over. 'What, like this?'

'It's what we planned.'

She took his hand and followed him outside to a small frozen-over pond. Her feet were snuggled inside padded white skates, and her long dress was cropped to above her ankles. Charlie's dark jacket had disappeared, leaving him with rolled shirt sleeves, revealing his forearms that Grace loved so much.

The air was mild and smelled like wood was burning close by. Fairy lights swayed from tree branches in the gentle breeze drifting by every so often, and a fluffed-up robin was perched on a large boulder the other side of the pond. It chirped, gaining her attention.

'Be happy, Gracie,' said the bird, sounding oddly like her grandfather, who had recently passed away. 'Wake up and enjoy your life. The dark days are over. You can fly now, so you spread those beautiful wings of yours and take to the sky with that man.'

Charlie swirled her around on the solid ice whilst singing 'Tiny Dancer' out loud and laughing in between lyrics, but all Grace could hear was the voice of the robin, telling her one last time to wake up.

30

Charlie

This isn't happening. Not again. Not to Grace. Not to us.

Charlie paced the hospital room where his wife slept peacefully, with a patched-up head wound and her whole family surrounding her.

'That was Viv,' said Ashley, gesturing towards her phone. 'She said Ewan is at the police station.'

'Good bloody job,' snapped Harriet. 'I hope they lock him up and throw away the key.'

'He hasn't been arrested. They're just talking to him to find out what happened,' Ashley added.

Lexi reached over and gently patted Harriet's arm. 'Hal, how's Tommy bearing up?'

'Jude took him home. He's okay, I think. He was so worried about Grace last time, his grades started dropping. His teacher called me in to discuss it.'

'I didn't know that,' said Fiona, frowning over at Harriet.

'I didn't want to worry you, Mum. You had enough on your plate.'

Lexi sighed deeply. 'It's hard for little kids. They don't understand. Mind you, I didn't understand half of what was going on with our Grace.' She turned to her dad, tears filling her eyes. 'Oh God, what are we going to do this time?'

'Nothing,' said Kerri. 'Grace is fine. She just banged her head. That's all. She'll wake up in a minute.'

'You said that last time,' said Molly.

Kerri huffed as she shrugged. 'Yes, well, this time is different. The doctor gave her a head scan and the all clear. That's good, right?' She looked to Charlie for confirmation.

All eyes were on him, waiting for his expert opinion, but Charlie suddenly felt useless, as though he had never taken any medical courses.

Don't ask me anymore. I don't know what's happening to my wife. One moment she's healing, the next, we're right back here.

He nodded. It was all he had the energy to do.

Ashley clutched her phone in her hands. 'I'm going to kill Ewan when I see him. What the hell was he even doing with Grace down by the lake?'

'The police are dealing with him, love,' said Fiona. She swallowed hard, as her voice had broken mid-sentence.

Ronnie placed one hand over hers whilst his other remained upon Grace's. 'I'll deal with him, Fee.'

'You won't,' she snapped. 'I'm not having you getting arrested because of him. That man has caused our family enough hurt.'

'We don't know what happened yet,' said Kerri. 'All we know is he was there.'

'Can we change the subject, please?' Molly shook her head at them all. 'Grace needs some positive vibes around her. She can probably hear us, you know. And she doesn't need to stress or get more of a headache.'

Ashley linked arms with Kerri. 'Molly's right, we need a timeout. Come on, let's go to the canteen and have a coffee. Grace needs peace and quiet.' She gestured towards Charlie. 'Charlie will call us if anything changes.'

Fiona was reluctant to move and had to be practically lifted from her chair by Lexi and Harriet. 'Ten minutes, then I'll be back,' she told Charlie on her way out.

Charlie inhaled deeply and flopped down into the big blue chair by Grace's side. He lowered his head to her hand and took another calming breath, trying hard to steady his nerves and settle his racing heart. Grace's family weren't the only ones who wanted to get their hands on Ewan.

Why now? Why us? What did we ever do to deserve this? Oh, Grace, honey, I love you so much. When you were under that water, I... I... I can't think about it.

He moved his face so his lips could press down on her pale knuckles. He leaned up and straightened the top part of her hospital gown and smiled warmly at her peaceful face. Her right cheek was slightly bruised, and her eyebrow was grazed, but apart from that, she looked okay.

'I just want to climb in bed with you and hold you all night,' he whispered close to her face.

'What's stopping you?'

Charlie shot up. His wide eyes gazed down into her sleepy ones. 'Grace?'

Grace smiled, then winced. 'Ooh, my head hurts.' She went to touch the dressing, but Charlie took her hand.

'You knocked your head. Again. Seems to be your thing.'

'Am I all right?'

'You tell me.'

'I feel fine, just a bit bruised in places.'

'Well, you did take a fall.'

'Who are you?'

Charlie's heart disappeared. 'What?' he just about managed to say, as a lump was stuck in his throat.

Grace snorted a quiet laugh, then winced. 'Just kidding. I know exactly who you are, Hot Doc.'

He pulled in his lips and shook his head. 'Really? You wanna play that game now?' He smiled at her bad sense of humour. 'Please don't do that to me, honey. I can't take it again.' He gently stroked her cheek.

'Sorry,' she whispered, half smiling.

'Do you remember what happened before you fell off the bridge?'

Her brow crinkled as her eyes narrowed as though tired. 'I remember. Ewan grabbed my arms, telling me he still loved me. I tried to free myself, then I heard you shout, and Ewan released me. That's when I tumbled, then saw the water. That was it. He didn't push me or anything. I just slipped.' She tried to sit up, but Charlie settled her back against the plump pillows. 'Where is he?'

'Rest, honey. The police are questioning him. Everything is okay. You just need to let your head heal, so stop trying to get up.'

'Charlie, come closer.' She rested her hand on his chest as he leaned over. 'My head is healed,' she whispered.

His smile widened to match hers. 'I know, Grace, but you have stitches. So just—'

'No. You don't understand. I remember, Charlie. I remember you.'

He gently brushed back her blood-stained hair that hadn't been fully cleaned. 'That's good to know. I think everyone was worried you might forget this last month. I know I thought it, so your joke didn't help just then.'

'You're not listening. I remember you, Hot Doc. All of it. Our whole life together. The snow, the Northern Lights, our first date, the talking snowman, even the robin. Ooh, Grandad. He was there. He told me to wake up and get on with my life.' Her fist balled his shirt. 'Charlie, my memory came back.'

Charlie wasn't looking as enthusiastic as her. 'Talking snowman?'

'I guess that part was a dream. I don't know. I don't care. All I know is, I remember you, Charlie Wallis. Isn't that wonderful?'

A rush of love, moonbeams, and all things amazing flooded him from head to toe. It wasn't possible for his smile to be any bigger. He lowered his face until his lips rested upon hers. 'Oh, Grace,' he mumbled.

'Charlie, I love you so much. Thank you for sticking by me.'

He felt every word vibrate against his skin. He pulled away to look her in the eyes. 'Don't thank me. I'll never leave you. Ever. Get that through your unpredictable head.' He nudged her nose with his own, then kissed her cheek. 'I love you so much.' He pulled away and sat by her side on the bed, holding her hand gently.

Grace smiled at him. 'Is everyone still at the party?'

'No. That got closed down. Your family are in the canteen, having a coffee. They'll be back in a minute. Ten, your mother assured me.' He breathed out a laugh. 'Won't they be in for a surprise.'

Grace tried to scratch around her dressing, but Charlie lowered her hand. 'Did they do the raffle beforehand?'

'Really, that's all you're thinking about?'

'I wanted to know if we won a prize.'

Charlie smiled and nodded. 'Oh, we won a prize, all right. The biggest prize, in fact.'

'Are you talking about my memory?'

'It was on my Santa's wish list.'

Grace giggled and placed his hand by her mouth. 'Mine too. I even placed one in Santa's letterbox at the castle when no one was looking.'

'Me too.' He winked, warming as she smiled.

'I guess wishes do come true.'

'Hey, it's Christmas. Miracle time.' He glanced at his watch. 'Actually, it's just gone midnight. Happy Christmas, Grace.'

'Merry Christmas, my lovely.'

They shared a gentle kiss before Charlie snuggled to her side on the single bed.

'So, tell me more about this talking snowman.'

Grace laughed. 'We made him in Lapland.'

'Oh, that guy.'

'He helped jog my memory.'

'I love him already.'

They turned their heads so they were facing each other. Grace smiled. 'A husky spoke to me too.'

'Sounds like my kind of place.'

'We're going back there soon. We can still do that, right?'

'Of course. We can make some new memories.'

Grace snuggled closer, and they smiled into each other's eyes. 'I just love making memories with you.'

* * *

If you enjoyed this story, come back to Pepper Bay and find out all about Vivien and Finn.

The Gatehouse Café

Vivien leads a double life. A happy one the world sees and a miserable one that's hidden away. Nobody knows what goes on in her home once she has closed up the café for the day. She doesn't think anyone will believe that her partner is a horrible person, especially as he is a policeman.

Finn has been secretly in love with Vivien since he was a teenager, but she's only ever viewed him as a friend. When he discovers she's in trouble at home, he does everything in his power to help set her free, because even if she never falls in love with him, she's still his best friend, and she needs help.

www.ingramcontent.com/pod-product-compliance
Lightning Source LLC
Chambersburg PA
CBHW031105080526
44587CB00011B/832